After Revival Comes

After Revival Comes

O. S. Hawkins

BROADMAN PRESS
Nashville, Tennessee

© Copyright 1981 • Broadman Press
All rights reserved.
4262-31
ISBN: 0-8054-6231-7

All Scripture quotations are from the *New American Standard
Bible.* Copyright © The Lockman Foundation, 1960, 1962, 1963,
1971, 1972, 1973, 1975. Used by permission.

Dewey Decimal Classification: 269
Subject heading: EVANGELISTIC WORK
Library of Congress Catalog Card Number: 81-66090

Printed in the United States of America

Dedication

These pages are dedicated to the glory of the Lord Jesus and the advancement of his kingdom with grateful appreciation for a multitude of undeserved blessings he has bestowed upon me, not the least of which is my wife, Susie. If I had to write down everything I ever hoped and prayed for in a wife, I would simply write what she is!

Table of Contents

Foreword

One of the great excitements of my ministry is to observe certain young men whom God has touched and upon whom rests his anointing. O. S. Hawkins is one of these.

After Revival Comes will prove to be a fitting sequel to his first book, *When Revival Comes*. Again, his ability to present the word of God in an appealing, fresh manner is obvious. O. S.'s church embodies what he preaches and writes and is the proving ground for these concepts from the Word of God, shared in the dynamic of the Holy Spirit. I happily and heartily commend this book to all who seek a blessing.

Jack R. Taylor

Introduction

It began like all the rest of those long and tiresome weeks. I was the young pastor of the thousand member First Baptist Church in Hobart, Oklahoma, and was at the same time taking eighteen hours in graduate school 230 miles away in Fort Worth.

I was busy in those days doing all I knew to do, studying hard at the seminary, and rushing back to the church field to tell people how to receive Jesus into their lives. To be quite honest, I couldn't tell them what to do with him once he came in because I had not discovered that myself. I thought the kingdom of God was advancing by my church becoming filled with people. I had no idea that it was really advanced by my people becoming filled with God.

Back to the beginning of the week. I set out for my usual 460-mile weekly round trip, spending the first hour of that early-morning drive doing what came naturally, feeling sorry for myself. After all, the sun had not risen as yet. I was not up on my reading assignments. I felt guilty leaving my church people, and most of all Susie and our new little daughter, Wendy (whom I hardly knew), were being left alone for four more days. Stephen had nothing on me. I was a modern-day martyr!

As I drove along that morning, the radio station began to

11

fade out. I remembered a tape given to me a few weeks earlier. It was a message by a "fanatical" Baptist preacher, Jack Taylor, who had been stirring up many people in those days with his messages on the Spirit-filled life. The tape had been securely hidden in the glove compartment of my car for weeks.

Being quite certain it was safe to listen without fear of my peers taking note, I placed it in my cassette recorder. Almost immediately, I sensed God was speaking directly to my stubborn, self-willed heart. He and I were beginning a divine appointment. The strongholds—pride, narrow-mindedness, tradition—all began to fall one by one. I drove until I could go no farther. I pulled over to the side of the road.

That early morning on Highway 70 outside of Wichita Falls, Texas, I dethroned the big "I" and enthroned the Lord Jesus in my heart. Suddenly, the whole world looked different. Oh, I didn't see any great light or vision but I know that the Holy Spirit filled my life that morning. I'm still not what I ought to be, but I've never been the same since the morning that revival came to my heart!

"Wilt thou not Thyself receive us again, That Thy people may rejoice in Thee?" (Ps. 85:6). These words of the psalmist express the cry of many of God's children today. I fear, however, that many of us who are praying for revival are really praying for an extension of our own affluence and prosperity. You know, the good ol' American way—hot dogs, apple pie, and a convenient Sunday-morning commitment that doesn't compel us to bear a cross. A lot of us preachers seem to be more interested in our public relations image, the "I-know-the-governor" syndrome, than we are in "weeping between the porch and the altar" (Joel 2:17) over the sins of our people.

We have been too long without a visitation from heaven. None of us have seen any nation trembling or cities shaking, nothing to compare to the Great Awakening, the Hebrides revival, or other such broad atmospheric visitations. But we can, and we must!

Why then the title, *After Revival Comes?* Because revival is, as defined by Stephen Olford in our earlier volume, *When*

Revival Comes, "that strange and sovereign work of God in which he visits his own people, restoring, reanimating, and releasing them into the fullness of his blessing." And this, dear friends, is happening today in the lives of thousands of people. These little brush fires are burning brightly, and one day the wind of the Holy Spirit is going to blow through and spread these fires into a blaze of revival in our churches and land.

As we begin our journey, let me remind you of what the Lord Jesus is doing right now. He is praying for you as you hold this volume in your hand. The Book of Hebrews tells us he "always lives to make intercession for us"(7:25).

Now let's hasten on to some exciting discoveries and see what happens in our own individual lives, *After Revival Comes.*

O. S. HAWKINS

Perspective

This is a volume for believers, those who have opened their hearts to receive Jesus and the free gift of eternal life. Revival always begins with God's own people. So this book is written to those who are saved.

However, if you have never accepted Jesus Christ as Savior, please don't put this book on the shelf now. This could be a moment of destiny for you, a place of beginning again, a divine appointment with God himself. With that in mind, this perspective is written that you may know Christ in the free pardon of sin and, in knowing him, be ready for the amazing adventure for which you were created, fellowshipping with God!

The Bible declares that the person who has not invited Christ into his life is lost. And Jesus came "to seek and to save that which was lost" (Luke 19:10). God takes the initiative; in fact, the Holy Spirit may be pointing you to Jesus right now. God made the plan of salvation so simple that a child can assimilate it. In fact, Jesus himself taught that if any of us were going to come after him, we must become like a little child, with simple, childlike faith.

Many think salvation is a matter of the head, how much one has to know intellectually before one can have eternal life.

But, if this were true, he wouldn't be a fair God. After all, some have higher I.Q.'s than others and can comprehend more than others. Others claim salvation is a matter of the hand, how much one has to do in order to be saved. Again, if this were true, he wouldn't be a fair God for some can do more than others. Jesus made salvation a matter of the heart. "For with the heart man believes, resulting in righteousness, and with the mouth he confesses, resulting in salvation" (Rom. 10:10).

God has done everything possible to save us. Jesus left the glories of heaven to become as helpless as a tiny baby, and thirty-three years later to be our sin-bearer on the cross, taking the punishment for our sins. And today, God sends his Spirit to convict us, convince us, and point us to Jesus. Salvation is not spelled d-o but d-o-n-e. Our part is to receive him!

Would you, reader, be willing to do that right now? How?

Acknowledge that you are a sinner and that you need Jesus. "For all have sinned and fall short of the glory of God" (Rom. 3:23). Jesus said, "Behold, I stand at the door and knock; if any one hears My voice and opens the door, I will come into him, and will dine with him, and he with Me" (Rev. 3:20).

Accept him by asking him to forgive you of your sin and to change your mind (repentance) about the way of salvation. "He who confesses and forsakes [his transgressions] will find compassion" (Prov. 28:13). Invite him into your heart right now. "But as many as received Him, to them He gave the right to become children of God, even to those who believe in His name" (John 1:12).

Affirm that you are saved. "That if you confess with your mouth Jesus as Lord, and believe in your heart that God raised Him from the dead, you shall be saved; for with the heart man believes, resulting in righteousness, and with the mouth he confesses, resulting in salvation" (Rom. 10:9-10). It may be that you will not feel anything until you say something. If you asked him to come in, go ahead and say it, out loud, "Jesus is alive in *me*!"

Now this volume is for you. Join us as we see what happens *After Revival Comes.*

AUTHOR'S NOTE

At the beginning of each chapter is a brief personal story. Each relates a true-life experience from within the context of a genuine revival atmosphere. Because every person in reality is a microcosm of the larger group to which they belong, it is both interesting and productive to view the individual happenings. May God bless these to your enjoyment and edification.

Death Unto Life . . . Literally!

He was a black kid from the streets, twenty-one years old, and far away from his Newark, New Jersey, home. He had tried it all. Let your imagination run loose, and all you could imagine would be evident in Todd's broken life. He seemed to be on a merry-go-round, finding it virtually impossible to break with his frantic life. He couldn't get his wants together and didn't know how to break free if his desires had been unanimous.

At this point, Roy crossed the path of Todd. Roy got up before the rest of us on Sunday morning and drove a van to the beach to pick up runaways to bring them to Jesus. Todd immediately sensed Roy's genuine concern and hopped in for a ride. At church that morning Todd saw something he had never seen, people who genuinely cared and loved him, regardless of his color or his life-style. It was the love of Jesus constraining Todd!

Edd took an interest and stayed an hour after church, sharing with Todd the wonderful plan of salvation, and Todd accepted Jesus as his own personal Savior and Lord! David got into the act. He gave Todd a Bible and helped him in growing spiritually. Todd's life was changed. He was in every service with his open Bible and taking notes of the messages. He was thirsting for the truths of God!

Some time ago Todd was killed in an auto accident. Weep not, he is with Jesus. Todd is free today, and forever.

When the shocking news reached me, my first impulse was to thank God for our church. Too many churches spend the majority of their time on the peripheral matters—arguing over what color the carpet ought to be or what department gets what piano, or picking apart the budget! God is blessing us because Jesus is Lord, and we are interested in what Jesus was interested in—"seeking to save that which was lost" (Luke 19:10). What if Roy hadn't cared enough to get up early? What if Edd had been more concerned about getting to lunch than sharing the gospel? What if David hadn't taken a personal interest? What if—what if—what if? Take your rest, Todd, we will join you soon. We are awaiting our "blessed hope and the appearing of the glory of our great God and Savior, Christ Jesus" (Titus 2:13).

We must never lose sight of being soul seekers. Out there in that high-rise condominium is a widow, lonely and lost. Over in that poverty-stricken neighborhood is a little family with heartache, too poor for most high-steeple, stained-glass, brick churches to be after, but needy and lost. Inside that jail cell, a sin-sick man is marking "X's" across each day of his calendar, waiting, lost. Behind the iron gates of that big home on the water is a family with unbelievable problems, desperately in need of Jesus. Down on the Fort Lauderdale strip is a little fourteen-year-old runaway girl selling her body to make it through another day. She needs Jesus. Soul seekers, that's us when we are most like Jesus.

Andrew found Peter. Jesus found Philip. Philip found Nathanael. Roy found Todd. This is a sure sign of revival. People are swept into the kingdom of God by the witness of those caught up in the Spirit, after revival comes.

Chapter 1
BEING BEFORE DOING

CHAPTER 1
Being Before Doing
(Matthew 5:3-10)

I. The Pathway Toward the Victorious Life (vv. 3-5)

    A. Commences with an awareness of our destitute condition
"Blessed are the poor in spirit" (v. 3);

    B. Continues with an attitude of desperate concern
"Blessed are those who mourn" (v. 4);

    C. Consummates with an acceptance of divine control
"Blessed are the gentle [meek]" (v. 5).

II. The Passageway into the Victorious Life (v. 6)

    "Blessed are those who hunger and thirst for righteousness"
(v. 6).

III. The Proofs Issuing Out of the Victorious Life (vv. 7-10)

    A. A concern which is humane
"Blessed are the merciful" (v. 7).

    B. A character which is holy
"Blessed are the pure in heart" (v. 8).

    C. A conduct which is harmonious
"Blessed are the peacemakers" (v. 9).

    D. A comprehension which is heavenly
"Blessed are those who have been persecuted for the sake of
righteousness" (v. 10).

Being Before Doing

Blessed are the poor in spirit, for theirs is the kingdom of heaven.

Blessed are those who mourn, for they shall be comforted.

Blessed are the gentle, for they shall inherit the earth.

Blessed are those who hunger and thirst for righteousness, for they shall be satisfied.

Blessed are the merciful, for they shall receive mercy.

Blessed are the pure in heart, for they shall see God.

Blessed are the peacemakers, for they shall be called sons of God,

Blessed are those who have been persecuted for the sake of righteousness, for theirs is the kingdom of heaven (Matt. 5:3-10).

It was a new and eye-opening experience for the Hawkins family—Fort Lauderdale, Florida, U.S.A., in the heart of the fastest-growing county on the entire North American continent! The fast-paced, hustle-bustle, bumper-to-bumper traffic of over one million people, all seemingly in a hurry, was far from Ada, the quiet little Oklahoma town which we had called home only one week earlier. And it was even farther from our first pastorate in Hobart, Oklahoma. I remember the front-page headlines and all the commotion the day the one traffic light at the town square (incidentally, the only traffic light in town) went on the blink!

Needless to note, the Hawkins four were filled with mixed emotion as we suddenly found ourselves in a sea of humanity. All our friends were 1,400 miles away. Gone were the days of a leisurely afternoon drive or a quick trip out to the local ranch to ride horses or climb mountains. But we soon found plenty of benefits, like making new friends in our new church. And after all, there were the beach, the ocean, swimming pools galore, and, most importantly for Wendy and Holly, there seemed to be a McDonald's on every corner. Little did we realize the Lord was using those early days of transition to teach us a valuable lesson that would shape the course of our entire lives and bring mercy drops of revival to thousands.

It all happened late one afternoon. I had just gone through "one of those days" at the office. Susie, my wife, had done double duty all day long. Have you ever tried to arrange things in a new house, unpack boxes, and referee two little girls trying to beat boredom and adjust to their new surroundings? We made a unanimous decision. We were going out for dinner!

Everything was going well until we reached a major intersection. While waiting at the traffic light, Holly looked to the right and saw the golden arches. Suddenly, I found myself in a headlock as from the back seat she began to shout, "Daddy, Daddy, turn right, turn right! Let's go to McDonald's!" At about the same time Wendy had been looking out her back window and to the left saw Mario's Pizza. The barrage on my back suddenly intensified as now in my other ear I began to hear a not-so-melodious four-year-old voice blasting, "No, Daddy, turn left. I want to go eat pizza!"

As though that were not enough, Susie then informed me she wanted to head straight down the street to the cafeteria where she could eat a spinach salad! It all happened in a flash—battle royal, indecision, light turned green, horns began to blow, the man behind me began to shake his fist . . . I learned a few new words from him, and, you guessed it, I lost my cool! After all the confusion, we went home and ate peanut butter sandwiches.

Though the experience was gruesome, the end was glorious; not the peanut butter sandwiches, but the never-to-be-forgotten lesson. Since then we have never left our driveway until we have decided where we are going. It is amazing how much smoother, quieter, and more digestible our evening meals have become. By determining our destination before we leave, we always know where to turn when we reach an intersection.

It was all coming together. This is a vital principle in the Christian life. Every day we are confronted with intersections. From every side there is pressure to turn in a certain direction. As if little children were screaming in our ears, we are left with indecision and then, suddenly the light changes and we have to move. Too often, too many of us have made a wrong turn under such adverse circumstances. It is important to decide where to turn before we reach the intersection. In fact, it is the only way to travel.

This is what I mean: being comes before doing, for what we do will be determined by who and what we are! In a real sense the issue is not revival. The actual issue is for us to discover, or perhaps rediscover, who Jesus in truth is and what our position is in him! For when we "are" who we are supposed to be, our doing will no longer be a matter of drudgery, but will be as natural as water running downhill. Do not misunderstand. Being does not eliminate doing; being accelerates doing!

I am convinced that this is exactly what Jesus was trying to teach us when he began the greatest sermon ever preached with the Beatitudes (Matt. 5:3-12). Contrary to what many may think, the Beatitudes are not a set of rules, but instead they stand before us as a beautiful picture of the principle of *being before doing*. Let us look and learn from them as Jesus reveals the *pathway* toward this victorious life, the *passageway* into this victorious life, and finally, the *proofs* issuing out of this life of victory.

THE PATHWAY TOWARD THE
VICTORIOUS LIFE
(Matt. 5:3-5)

As we start on this pathway, we quickly find that our first step *commences with an awareness of our destitute condition* (v. 3). In the words of Jesus, "Blessed are the poor in spirit, for theirs is the kingdom of heaven." We will understand nothing of being before doing, and we will not begin in the direction of the victorious life, until we initially realize our totally abject spiritual poverty. We are hopeless, helpless, spiritually poverty-stricken apart from Jesus Christ. There is no good in us. The Scriptures remind us that the very best of us are as "filthy rags" when placed alongside the righteousness of Jesus.

There is a tremendous paradox here. "Blessed [happy] are the poor in spirit." What a contrast to the philosophies of the world that bombard us and our children from the media. Friend, the only way to true happiness is through Jesus Christ, and the only way to Jesus Christ is through the emptying of the "old self."

Secular humanism, the godless philosophy circulated by today's vocal minority, is trying to change the wording of this first Beatitude. Humanists are telling us that happiness comes in our self-sufficiency. They say, "Jesus should have said, 'Blessed are the self-sufficient.' " But they are wrong. Miserable are the self-sufficient! Exceedingly happy, blessed, are those who realize their spiritual poverty apart from the Lord Jesus! This is the first step to victory. It commences with an awareness of our destitute condition.

Along this pathway, there is a second step. It *continues with an attitude of destitute concern.* Jesus expressed it in the second Beatitude: "Blessed are those who mourn, for they shall be comforted." It is not enough simply to realize we are poverty-stricken spiritually. In order to "be," we must come to the place where we mourn over our desperate condition. Once we catch a glimpse of the holiness of God, it is inevitable that we will mourn over our own spiritual poverty.

Again we see a paradox. "Happy are they that mourn"? How does this bring happiness? What a contrast this is to the world's philosophy. The truth is, when a person reaches the place where he is burdened about his spiritual condition, repentance is immediately around the corner, and that is the place of true happiness.

The secularists of today are also trying to change the wording of the second Beatitude. In the place of the words of Jesus, "Happy are those who mourn," they rewrite it to read, "Happy are the self-satisfied." But again they are dead wrong. Miserable are the self-satisfied! Blessed, happy, are those who are aware of their destitute condition and have an attitude of desperate concern.

What about you? Does it bother you, your neglect, your cold-heartedness? You will never experience victory until you take these first two steps. The pathway toward the victorious life is like any other pathway in that we can only take one step at a time. Are you still with me? If so, we have taken two giant steps together, and now we are ready for a third step which carries us to the door of the victorious life.

This pathway *consummates with an acceptance of divine control.* In the words of Jesus, "Blessed are the gentle [meek]." To be meek is to have a broken will and a receptive heart before God. Along this pathway it is not enough merely to realize our spiritual poverty, or even to reach the place of mourning over our neglect. We must go one step further to come under the control of our Master. At this step, being becomes a reality. The Greek word *proas* in this third Beatitude is the same word used for an animal which has been domesticated. The word-picture describes a wild animal who is trained to obey the command of his master, who accepts control, and whose will is broken to the master's will. Thus, Jesus is plainly saying, "Happy are those who come under the control of the Master."

At this writing we are seeing this truth unfold in our home. One month ago we had an addition to our family. At long last, there is another male at our house. His name is

"Rags," and he is a miniature dachshund puppy. Before our eyes we are watching his will being broken to our will. Now, like the rest of us, he has a long way to go! He is only about 50 percent housebroken, but he is making progress. He knows to come when we call him. He lies down when we tell him to. He is coming under the control of his master. And this is exactly what Jesus is teaching in this text, "Happy are those who come under the control of their master."

There is yet another paradox found here. "Happy are the meek"? Yes, for here is a man who has learned the joy of trusting Jesus Christ with every area and detail of his life.

But again the humanists come knocking at our door with, "Happy are the self-willed." They are telling us that true happiness is only achieved in attaining our human potential. But they are wrong. Miserable are the self-willed! Happy, blessed, are the meek, those who have surrendered their will to God's will.

Is the will of God being done in your life? Have you walked these three steps down this pathway to victory? Jesus did! As always, he is our example. He prayed much. He realized full well how the "flesh profits nothing" (John 6:63). His journey continued with an attitude of desperate concern. He was a man of sorrows, acquainted with grief. Listen to him as he mourned in Gethsemane's garden. His journey consummated with an acceptance of divine control. He said he had come to do "the will of Him who sent Me" (John 5:30). He finished his pathway to victory as he prayed, "Yet, not My will, but Thine be done" (Luke 22:42).

These three pivotal steps lead us to the door of the victorious life, and the next Beatitude leads us inside. Note secondly:

THE PASSAGEWAY INTO THE
VICTORIOUS LIFE
(Matt. 5:6)

What is this righteousness? It is a desire to be free from sin because sin separates us from God. It is a longing to be holy, to be what God intends us to be. The word found here in this fourth Beatitude has to do with hungering after the whole loaf of bread or thirsting after the entire pitcher of water. It is not content with a piece of the loaf or a taste of the water. It carries with it a spirit of conquest. Jesus is again saying, in essence, "Blessed are those who hunger and thirst for the whole of righteousness, for total righteousness, for complete righteousness."

Please note: We are not to hunger and thirst after happiness. This is what the world's crowd is doing today, driving at breakneck speed looking for happiness, never seeming to find it, and finding out too late they are on a dead-end street. The truth is, happiness is never something that should be directly sought. It is always something that results from seeking something else. More about that in a moment.

Here again we discover a fourth paradox. "Blessed are those who hunger and thirst"? What a contrast to the world's standard. Blessed are those who hunger and thirst after what? Wealth? Money? Status? Position? Popularity? No! Not at all. Happy are those who are seeking after righteousness. And note, it is not "Happy are those which have," but "Happy are those who hunger and thirst." Christ pronounces as blessed not those who are *full* of righteousness, but those who *hunger* and *thirst* after righteousness. "Blessed are those who hunger and thirst for righteousness, for they shall be satisfied." The Christian is one who is hungering and thirsting and yet, at the same time, is satisfied. And the truth is, the more one is filled, the more one is satisfied, and the more one is hungering and thirsting!

Here comes that humanist again. It is obvious by now he is out to pervert once again the words of Jesus. What is that he is shouting now? Oh yes, we hear him from every side shouting, "Happy are the self-righteous!" Well, we have some more news for him. Miserable are the self-righteous! "Happy are those who hunger and thirst for righteousness, for they shall be satisfied."

Yielding to the lordship of Christ, being controlled by the

Holy Spirit, is the passageway into victory. And incidentally, the proof that one is being filled with the Holy Spirit is not to be found in the gifts of the Spirit, but in the fruit of the Spirit, which is "love, joy, peace, patience, kindness, goodness, faithfulness, gentleness, self-control; against such things there is no law" (Gal. 5:22-23). Jesus did not say, "By this shall all men know that you are my disciples if you raise the sick, or prophesy, or speak in tongues." What he said was, "By this all men will know that you are My disciples, if you have love for one another" (John 13:35). The only place that gifts receive a lengthy discourse in the Bible is in 1 Corinthians 12 to 14, and a careful reading will reveal not one word about the fullness of the Holy Spirit.

In today's Christian vocabulary, we have perverted a precious New Testament word, *charismatic*. It might interest you to realize that you are a charismatic! That is, if you have the Lord Jesus as your personal Savior. The word comes from two Greek words, *charis* and *mata*, which mean "grace gift" or "gift of grace." And the Scriptures are clear that all who are born again have some gift. Therefore a saved person is obviously a charismatic in the purest sense.

Today some people have developed "charismania," giftmadness. It becomes for them a crusade to make sure everyone gets "it." (I still am trying to find out what "it" is!) The Giver is neglected for the gift, and the gift becomes the end in itself. It often develops that the criteria for fellowship are determined by whether or not one has a certain gift. Those suffering from charismania need to become true charismatics.

But there is the other side of this coin, which is equally dangerous. Some people are suffering from "charisphobia," gift fear. Let someone mention a gift of the Holy Spirit, and these anemic sufferers shudder in fear, put up their shields, and often react with lovelessness. Those suffering from charisphobia need to realize they often quench the Spirit of a Holy God, and they need to become true charismatics.

Have you started on the pathway? The longest journey begins with the first step, and step one is to realize our spiritual poverty apart from Jesus Christ. Have you taken step two by getting to the place of burden and breaking? If so, it is a short step which follows, coming under the control of our Master, the Lord Jesus. This transports us to the passageway where we enter in by faith by our "hunger and thirst for righteousness."

How does one know when one is being filled with God's Spirit? Finally, let us observe some:

THE PROOFS ISSUING OUT OF THE VICTORIOUS LIFE
(Matt. 5:7-10)

The first proof that a person is being controlled by God's Spirit is *a concern which is humane*. In the words of Jesus, "Blessed are the merciful." Here is the great evidence that one has discovered the principle of being before doing. Having received mercy from the Lord, one now releases mercy to others. One has a genuine concern for others.

Recorded for all posterity is the story of the healing of the blind man at Bethsaida. Jesus was passing by and there was brought to him a man who could not see. Tenderly, yet determinedly, Jesus touched him and said, "Do you see now?" The man replied, "I see! But . . . I see men like trees walking." Jesus touched him again and asked, "Now what do you see?" Quickly came the reply, "I see every man clearly!"

At first touch, the man said, "I can see, but I can't tell who's who!" So blurred was this man's vision that he couldn't tell a man from a tree. He couldn't tell if the man was wearing a coat. He couldn't tell if the man was bald or had a full head of hair. By the way, there were some other things he couldn't see in that condition. He couldn't see a back if it were bent under a burden. He couldn't see lips if they were quivering. He couldn't see clothes if they were ragged and frayed. He couldn't see a stomach if it was bloated from malnutrition. He couldn't see feet if they were bare. He couldn't see a face if it was dirty. He couldn't see eyes if they were tearful.

Consequently, if he couldn't see tearful eyes, he couldn't

wipe the eyes of a tearful man. If he couldn't see a dirty face, he couldn't clean the face of the dirty man. If he couldn't see bare feet, he couldn't provide shoes for the shoeless man. If he couldn't see a bent back, he couldn't lighten a load or bear a burden.

Need I say more? Too many of us are only interested in *my* job, or *my* church, or *my* family, or *my* pain, me, me, me, mine, mine, mine, ours, ours, ours! We are no different from the man in Bethsaida. We see men without really seeing them. But when Jesus touches us, when we walk through the passageway of victory, the first proof is a concern for others. We will no longer see "men as trees walking."

I remind myself before stepping into the pulpit at each service that I am not preaching to a congregation. The First Baptist Church in Fort Lauderdale is a group of individuals with heartaches and burdens and needs. Oz and Alice sit on the third row on the west side of the auditorium every week. Their little daughter, Robin, is the same age as our little Wendy. But Oz and Alice have heard the doctor say to them, "Your little daughter has cystic fibrosis." They have burdens and needs and heartaches that I do not know anything about.

Nora sits on the second row on the east side of the building in every service. She has been sitting there for fifty years. The only difference is she sits there today without J. J., her husband of a half-century. He recently went to be with Jesus. She has heartaches and burdens I do not know anything about. Jim is there at every service, sitting with his two young boys. He is raising them alone. His wife deserted him. He works hard ten hours a day and then comes home and buries his life in his boys. He has heartaches and burdens that I do not know anything about.

Florence sits in the middle section of our auditorium at every service. For years she has been a backbone in our Sunday School and mission work. Just the other day, her doctor looked her in the face and said, "Florence, you have cancer!" She has heartaches and burdens I do not know anything about. Friend, we do not minister to congregations. We minister to individuals with burdens and needs. And if you are wondering whether you have "arrived" at personal revival, the first glaring proof is a deep concern for others. "Blessed are the merciful!"

You show me a person who is not genuinely concerned for others and I will show you a person who has not entered into or even headed toward the victorious life. On the other hand, show me a person who has taken the three steps along the pathway and entered the passageway into victory, and I will show you a person who is merciful.

The second proof issuing out of this victorious life is *a character which is holy.* In the words of Jesus, "[Happy] are the pure in heart." Too many today are resting on a head-religion supposing that all is well as long as their creed is sound. Too many others are resting on a hand-religion busily engaged in what they call Christian service. But the Lord looks upon the heart. "Blessed are the pure in heart." All the head-religion and hand-religion in the world will not save us. It is with the "heart that man believes, resulting in righteousness" (Rom. 10:10).

You show me a person who does not have a pure heart, who is living in sin, whose heart is stained, and I will show you a person who is not walking on the pathway toward victorious Christian living. On the other hand, you show me a person who has taken the three steps and entered into the passageway, and I will show you a person with a pure heart. It is an inevitable proof.

What about your heart? Is it pure? Or is it filled with lust, or conceit, or filth? At night, when all the lights are out and you are lying in bed, what do you think of? What surfaces in your mind at that time is what is filling your heart.

A third proof issuing out of the victorious life is *a conduct which is harmonious.* "Blessed are the peacemakers, for they shall be called sons of God." It is interesting that the Lord Jesus has pronounced this blessing on the "peacemakers" and not the "peace-lovers." This is an active expression, not a passive one. These are the promoters of unity who are blessed.

And note the accompanying promise—"they shall be called the sons of God." It does not say that they shall be "made" the sons of God, but "called" the sons of God. They are recognized as being in the image of God!

You show me a person who is trying to cause discord, who does not love his brothers and sisters in the Lord—that is, one who is not a peacemaker—and I will show you someone who has not entered into, much less walked upon, the pathway of the victorious life. On the other hand, point out someone who is walking in victory, and I will show you a peacemaker, promoting unity in the family of God.

Do people call you a child of God because you are a peacemaker? We simply cannot be controlled by God's Spirit without its resulting in a concern which is humane, a character which is holy, and a conduct which is harmonious.

There is a final proof of our being before doing, and it is *a comprehension which is heavenly.* "Blessed are those who have been persecuted for the sake of righteousness, for theirs is the kingdom of heaven. Blessed are you when men revile you, and persecute you, and say all kinds of evil against you falsely, on account of Me. Rejoice, and be glad, for your reward in heaven is great, for so they persecuted the prophets who were before you."

One of the proofs which always issues out of the victorious life is opposition and persecution. It has been true of every great servant of God, and, of course, true of Jesus himself. The Bible reminds us that "all who desire to live godly in Christ Jesus will be persecuted" (2 Tim. 3:12). Those who have walked the pathway and entered the passageway comprehend this, seeing opposition and problems for what they are—the strengthening of our faith.

What a paradox we have here. "Blessed [happy] are they who are persecuted " What a contrast to the world's standards. And why are we happy? Because we are thankful to God for the high honor he confers upon us in making us partakers of his suffering.

Show me a person who is never confronted with any sort

of criticism or persecution "for the sake of righteousness," and I will show you a person who has never stepped into victory, much less started in its direction. On the other hand, see a person who has surrendered to Jesus and is seeking righteousness, and I will show you a person who will rub the world the wrong way. We must not expect this world which so viciously crucified our Lord to receive us with open arms when we become like Him! Here is a comprehension which is heavenly.

Incidentally, would you like to know how to make people (in the average church) mad? Simply enter the church with a big smile on your face, open the hymnal, and enjoy belting out a stately congregational hymn; speak to several people, smiling all the while, and then give the preacher a few hearty "Amens" or a couple of "Praise the Lords," and you will have most of the congregation hopping mad at you before the service is completed!

It is strategic for us to note that the Beatitudes begin and end with the same promise, "for theirs is the kingdom of heaven" (Matt. 5:3,10). The Lord wants to show us that we belong to another kingdom. We are living in two worlds. We are in this world, but we are not of it. Our citizenship is in heaven where also we look for the Savior, the Lord Jesus Christ.

And on our journey toward the consummation, it is essential that we learn the importance of being before doing so when we come to those inevitable intersections, we will have already decided which way to turn. Remember the pathway. It commences with an awareness of our destitute condition, continues with an attitude of desperate concern, and consummates with an acceptance of divine control. This takes us to the passageway into the victorious life, and how do we know if we are there? There are proofs issuing out of the victorious life: a concern which is humane, a character which is holy, a conduct which is harmonious, and a comprehension which is heavenly.

"Blessed are those who hunger and thirst for righteousness, for they shall be satisfied" (Matt. 5:6).

A NEW CREATURE IN CHRIST JESUS

She had no church affiliation, and her existence held no place for God as she came by the church one day. She was broken and had reached the bottom. Between sobs Michelle began to pour out the details of her wrecked life. She was against a wall. Trying to raise a family of teenagers without a husband would be enough in itself. Upon hearing the gospel, Michelle opened her wounded life to receive the healing life of the resurrected Lord. He immediately began to make a difference!

About a week later Michelle came by again, obviously under a heavy burden. She related her story. A few weeks before Michelle's conversion, her daughter's life had been tragically snuffed out. She was a dancer in a topless night club in a rough area of our city. Michelle had not discouraged this, and like so many other tragic young people, her daughter had become mixed up and messed up with the wrong crowd.

That morning Michelle asked the most penetrating question I've ever heard. "Pastor, what right do I have to go to heaven when I allowed my daughter to slip out into eternity without any assurance?" Wendy, our precious little six-year-old had just been saved. The Lord gave the answer to Michelle that day. She had the same right my little Wendy did—none! None of us deserve this great salvation, but through God's grace, we get what we don't deserve and through his mercy we don't get what we do deserve.

By the way, Michelle and her family are growing by leaps and bounds and bringing many people to Jesus along the way. God is meeting their needs and healing their hearts.

All the "doing" in the world is not as important as "being," *after revival comes*

Chapter 2
OVERCOMING OBSTACLES

CHAPTER 2
Overcoming Obstacles
(Joshua 6:1-21)

I. The Unknown Becomes Known Through Communion (1-5)

"Now Jericho was tightly shut because of the sons of Israel; no one went out and no one came in.
"And the Lord said to Joshua, 'See I have given Jericho into your hand' " (vv. 1-2).

II. The Unbelievable Becomes Believable Through Compliance (6-19)

"So Joshua the son of Nun, called the priests and said to them, 'Take up the ark of the covenant, and let seven priests carry seven trumpets of rams' horns before the ark of the Lord.'
"Then he said to the people, 'Go forward, and march around the city, and let the armed men go on before the ark of the Lord' " (vv. 6-7).

III. The Impossible Becomes Possible Through Confidence (20-21)

"So the people shouted, and priests blew the trumpets; and it came about, when the people heard the sound of the trumpet, that the people shouted with a great shout and the wall fell down flat, so that the people went up into the city, every man straight ahead, and they took the city" (v 20).

Overcoming Obstacles

Now Jericho was tightly shut because of the sons of Israel; no one went out and no one came in.

And the Lord said to Joshua, "See, I have given Jericho into your hand, with its king and the valiant warriors.

"And you shall march around the city, all the men of war circling the city once. You shall do so for six days.

"Also seven priests shall carry seven trumpets of rams' horns before the ark; then on the seventh day you shall march around the city seven times, and the priests shall blow the trumpets.

"And it shall be that when they make a long blast with the ram's horn, and when you hear the sound of the trumpet, all the people shall shout with a great shout; and the wall of the city will fall down flat, and the people will go up every man straight ahead."

So Joshua the son of Nun called the priests and said to them, "Take up the ark of the covenant, and let seven priests carry seven trumpets of rams' horns before the ark of the Lord."

Then he said to the people, "Go forward, and march around the city, and let the armed men go on before the ark of the Lord."

And it was so, that when Joshua had spoken to the people, the seven priests carrying the seven trumpets of rams' horns before the Lord went forward and blew the trumpets;

and the ark of the covenant of the Lord followed them.

And the armed men went before the priests who blew the trumpets, and the rear guard came after the ark, while they continued to blow the trumpets.

But Joshua commanded the people, saying, "You shall not shout nor let your voice be heard, nor let a word proceed out of your mouth, until the day I tell you, 'Shout!' Then you shall shout!"

So he had the ark of the Lord taken around the city, circling it once; then they came into the camp and spent the night in the camp.

Now Joshua rose early in the morning, and the priests took up the ark of the Lord.

And the seven priests carrying the seven trumpets of rams' horns before the ark of the Lord went on continually, and blew the trumpets; and the armed men went before them, and the rear guard came after the ark of the Lord, while they continued to blow the trumpets.

Thus the second day they marched around the city once and returned to the camp; they did so for six days.

Then it came about on the seventh day that they rose early at the dawning of the day and marched around the city in the same manner seven times; only on that day they marched around the city seven times.

And it came about at the seventh time, when the priests blew the trumpets, Joshua said to the people, "Shout! For the Lord has given you the city.

"And the city shall be under the ban, it and all that is in it belongs to the Lord; only Rahab the harlot and all who are with her in the house shall live, because she hid the messengers whom we sent.

"But as for you, only keep yourselves from the things under the ban, lest you covet them and take some of the things under the ban, so you would make the camp of Israel accursed and bring trouble on it.

"But all the silver and gold and articles of bronze and iron are holy to the Lord; they shall go into the treasury of the Lord."

So the people shouted, and priests blew the trumpets; and it came about, when the people heard the sound of the trumpet, that the people shouted with a great shout and the wall fell down flat, so that the people went up into the city, every man straight ahead, and they took the city.

And they utterly destroyed everything in the city, both man and woman, young and old, and ox and sheep and donkey, with the edge of the sword (Josh. 6:1-21).

A little boy, seated on a bus, was busily reading his Bible. At a particular stop along the route a man boarded the bus and took a seat next to the small lad. After a few blocks the man's curiosity finally got the best of him and he asked, "Is that a Bible you're reading?"

"Sure is," replied the boy.

"What are you reading about?"

"I'm reading the story of Joshua marching around the city of Jericho and the walls falling down."

The man began to chuckle. "Surely you don't believe that fable to be true," he replied.

"Most certainly!" assured the lad.

"Now, how do you know that's true?"

"Well," replied the boy, "When I get to heaven, I'll just go up to Joshua and ask him about it personally."

Again the man roared in disbelief, saying, "And what if Joshua is not there?"

Immediately came the boy's reply, "Then you can ask him!"

Not only is the story of Jericho's walls true, but it holds for us some valuable principles in the life of victory. After revival comes, it brings with it the continuing process of becoming an overcomer—not simply week by week or even day by day, but hour by hour and moment by moment. The classic example of this truth is found in this familiar story of Joshua and the walls of Jericho.

As you recall, the children of Israel had entered the land of blessing after years of wilderness wandering and years of Egyptian slavery. Jericho became for them the place where they had to decide whether they would go on with God in the face of tremendous obstacles or be content to retreat and live out their days in the wilderness with no real purpose or direction.

We all arrive there at some point, don't we? There comes for all of us some particular place or situation that demands of us to go on . . . or . . . turn back. The chapter before us deals with this exact matter. It teaches us how to overcome our obstacles. After all, none of us are immune to our Jericho walls that lurk before us as monstrous obstacles to victory. Let's go to Jericho and learn how to overcome obstacles. Remember, it is the place where we decide to go on—or turn back. How do we overcome our obstacles? Let's note initially:

THE UNKNOWN BECOMES KNOWN
THROUGH COMMUNION
(Josh. 6:1-5)

Upon entering the Promised Land of milk and honey, Joshua was faced with an unknown. The children of Israel had set foot in the Promised Land. At long last, after all those years of wandering and delay, they had reached their destination. But upon reaching it they were faced with a major obstacle—Jericho! And Joshua knew that if he could not go past Jericho, he could never possess the land God had given him.

What was so difficult about overcoming Jericho? There was the problem of reaching it. Jericho was encompassed by a wall. Not just "a" wall, but a great wall. Some commentators state that the wall encompassing Jericho was sixty feet high and thirty feet wide! Can you picture it? There it stood, towering that high and so thick that two or three chariots could be driven abreast around the top of it. It stood as a great Gibraltar glistening in the desert sun on the banks of the Jordan. What an obstacle! They could not climb it. They could not dig through it. They could not tunnel under it.

What was Joshua to do? How did this huge unknown become known to Joshua? The secret lies in Joshua 6:2. "*And the Lord said to Joshua,* 'See I have given Jericho into your hand, with its king and the valiant warriors.' "

A careful reading of the Book of Joshua will reveal the frequency of those words—"And the Lord said to Joshua." In chapter 1, verse 1, "That the Lord spoke to Joshua." In chapter 3, verse 7, "Now the Lord said to Joshua." In chapter 4, verse 1, "And the Lord spoke to Joshua." In chapter 4, verse 15, "And the Lord said to Joshua." In chapter 5, verse 2, "The Lord said to Joshua." And now again in chapter 6, verse 2, "And the Lord said to Joshua."

Joshua had a God who spoke to him, do you? Joshua lived in such close communion with God through prayer that he was able to be led by God. In short, the unknown became known through communion. Prayer is the key.

And what did God make known to Joshua? He made known his plan for taking the city! "And the Lord said to Joshua, 'See, I have given Jericho into your hand, with its king and the valiant warriors. And you shall march around the city, all the men of war circling the city once. You shall do so for six days. Also seven priests shall carry seven trumpets of rams' horns before the ark; then on the seventh day you shall march around the city seven times, and the priests shall blow the trumpets. And it shall be that when they make a long blast with the ram's horn, and when you hear the sound of the trumpet, all the people shall shout with a great shout; and the wall of the city will fall down flat, and the people will go up every man straight ahead' " (Josh. 6:2-5).

God said, "See!" "See what?" asked Joshua. "See, the city is yours, the walls are yours, the land is yours." The unknown becomes known through communion. Let's become close and personal for a moment. You can be honest with yourself briefly. After all, you are reading and no one is watching. Are you up against a wall? A wall so large that if you do not get around it, you cannot live the life of victory? Many of us are living with a wall, morning and night. We cannot seem to dig through it. We cannot seem to tunnel under it. We've plotted, we've planned, but we keep butting our heads against our wall. Incidentally, this may be the very reason some of us are soreheads!

What about your wall? Is it a wall of unbelief, a wall of circumstances, a wall of pride, a wall of reason, a wall of broken relationships, or any of a hundred other walls? Do you honestly want to know how to deal with it? The unknown becomes known through communion. Fellowship with God. He has a plan for you, a plan which will enable you to overcome obstacles. It is the same plan he revealed to Joshua.

After revival comes, prayer is a must in overcoming the obstacles that will seek to divert us. Prayer ushers in revival and prayer keeps us in revival. Not only is it the delivery room where the godly pains of conviction result in the birth of revival, prayer is the school where the ABC's of revival are learned, applied, and mastered. We will never be overcomers apart from prayer. We will never have the unknown made known except through communion.

I wish you could visit our lovely city. Someone has said there are only two kinds of people in all the world—those who live in Fort Lauderdale and those who wish they did! We are famous down here for our citrus.

In the backyard of the Hawkins's home are a number of different fruit trees. My favorite is our large grapefruit tree that produces the most juicy, delectable grapefruit outside of Jericho itself. Every morning I go out, pull one off the tree, and squeeze some fresh fruit before breakfast. Do you realize where that grapefruit comes from? The hidden life of the tree! The secret of my grapefruit is in its roots. Its hidden life, what you do not see, produces what you do see! And so it is in overcoming obstacles. As the public life of a tree rests on the private life of its roots, so the public life of a man attempting to be an overcomer stands on his hidden life of communion with God. Learn a lesson from Joshua: in overcoming obstacles, the unknown becomes known through communion. As we follow the progression of our text, we note also:

THE UNBELIEVABLE BECOMES BELIEVABLE
THROUGH COMPLIANCE
(Josh. 6:6-19)

What did Joshua do? He complied with God's plan. He was obedient. Granted, it sounded ridiculous. It was unbelievable. But Joshua showed us that the believable becomes believable through compliance.

Note Joshua 6:6, "So Joshua the son of Nun called the priests and said to them, 'Take up the ark of the covenant and let seven priests carry seven trumpets of rams' horns before the ark of the Lord.' " Joshua did not understand it all, but he moved into action. He immediately called the priests together and gave them the game plan. He was obedient to God.

Now I want us to note something extremely important at this point. Why do you think God could use Joshua? Why is Joshua the picture to all of us of victorious Christian living? The answer lies in the fact that he did not argue with God and responded through obedience. We discover this all through the Book of Joshua. Joshua was obedient. He did as God commanded. In this case, he told the people what to do. Here was obedience.

Let's face it. This plan didn't make any sense. It sounded ridiculous. Who would believe that those massive walls would crumble in such a manner? After all, most of us pride ourselves on living by reason! Thank God Joshua didn't. Thank God he was obedient. He instructed the people as God commanded. He simply did as he was told. And when he did, the unbelievable became believable.

What did the people do? After all, this was totally against reason. "*And it was so,* that when Joshua had spoken to the people, the seven priests carrying the seven trumpets of rams' horns before the Lord went forward and blew the trumpets; and the ark of the covenant of the Lord followed them" (Josh. 6:8). God could work wonders among them because they were an obedient people. They didn't understand, but they walked.

They weren't certain what the result would be, but they walked. It was against reason, but they walked.

A casual reading of the text would most likely overlook a tremendously important word in verse 10 of this chapter. "But Joshua commanded the people saying, 'You shall not shout nor let your voice be heard, nor let a word proceed out of your mouth, until the day I tell you, "Shout!" Then you shall shout!' " (Josh. 6:10).

Now do you get the picture? As they walked they were not to open their mouths. Silence has a way of being golden, especially when the people of God are in obedience to Him. Why do you suppose Joshua issued such a strange command? It is not hard for most of us to see from our own experience what would happen if they had talked during those seven days. It wouldn't have been long before some negative spirit would have begun to doubt and would've said to the one next to him, "Man, we must be crazy! This is impossible! This is the most absurd thing I have ever heard of in my life! Look at those walls! There is no way! It is hot, dusty, I'm thirsty, I'm tired, seven days!"

No doubt his friend would have then begun to focus all of his attention on the wall itself. Doubt would have set in. Discouragement would have set in. Defeat would have set in. And before anyone realized it, doubt would have spread through the children of Israel's ranks like wildfire. It takes only a few negative people to quench the wonder-working power of God. Had God allowed them to talk, a few would have begun doubting, gossiping, speaking about the impossibility, reverting to reason, and the unity would have been severely damaged and victory lost. But thank God, recorded for all posterity is the fact that they were obedient to this command. And for them, the unbelievable became believable through compliance.

Incidentally, did you ever wonder why they had to march around that walled city so many times? After all, God is God. The walls could have fallen in one trip. Why then would God have them make fourteen trips? Every day for seven days they marched, not talking; just walking. Two hours per trip. Four-teen trips. Fifty-six long, hard looks at a side of that wall. Sixty feet high. Thirty feet wide.

God was deliberately delaying the victory so every Is-raelite would realize how utterly impossible it was for them to capture Jericho without divine help. They continued to walk until they died to every hope of conquest unless God inter-vened. And they walked until they came alive to the belief that God would indeed intervene. The more they walked, the more they believed. Here is the key! Some of us do not believe that the walls in our lives can crumble because we've never taken one step of obedience. The Israelites complied with God's plan. They were obedient and the unbelievable became believ-able through compliance.

We've seen what Joshua did. He was obedient. We've seen what the people did. They were obedient. They walked. Now, the question is: What will we do? Will we be obedient to God's call and trust totally in him to remove our wall, or will we keep on futilely trying to climb over it, dig under it, skirt around it, or perhaps continue to butt up against it?

Here is the point at which most of us fail to see our walls fall. Obedience is the key. God has called us to life on a higher plane, and too many of us are still clinging to reason. It's no wonder there's so little joy, so little victory. Obedience, obedi-ence, obedience—here is our answer. God may give you a plan (to overcome your wall) that is totally foreign to reason. Vic-tory will come for you only through your obedience.

Joshua had a task. It looked unbelievable. But he coupled that task with a vision, and it became believable as he obeyed God. Here is the dismal failure in the church today. Many churches have a task without a vision, and consequently the end result is drudgery with no spirit of conquest. We have all been there—working hard to complete our task—but void of any real joy or spirit of conquest. On the other side, there are churches that have a vision without a task, and consequently the end result is only a wishful dream. Most of us have been there too. A lot of talk about the possibilities of the future but no real walking around our walls when the test of obedience begins to shine on us. But thank God for what Joshua is trying to teach us—a vision *with* a task is the hope of our world! The unbelievable becomes believable through compliance.

I suppose our biggest difficulty in victorious Christian living is coming to the place where we admit our wall is too big for us—the place where, unless God intervenes, there is no pathway to victory. I believe that before God bestows a genuine blessing of victory, he will bring us to that place. It may be that God is allowing your wall to remain until you walk around it so much that you die to every hope of conquest unless he intervenes. Why not listen to the still, small voice of God in your heart right now? And simply do as you are told.

We have seen that the unknown becomes known through communion, the unbelievable becomes believable through compliance, and finally we turn our attention to the fact that

THE IMPOSSIBLE BECOMES POSSIBLE THROUGH CONFIDENCE
(Josh. 6:20-21)

Joshua had a deep confidence (faith) in God. When common sense said the situation was hopeless, Joshua had the uncommon sense to believe God could make the impossible possible. And He did! The impossible became possible through confidence.

Look at the outcome! After marching around those walls for seven days, Joshua gave the signal and the people shouted. And, then, . . the walls came tumbling down! They didn't fall in. They didn't fall out. They fell flat, and the children of Israel went over them and conquered the city! Would you like to hear something revealing? Our walls are not the problem. We are! The walls of Jericho were no problem for God, nor are ours. In fact, the main reason our walls loom so large before us is that we have a tendency to focus all of our attention on them. God merely wants us to praise him and be obedient, and he will take care of the walls, but not until we allow the impossible to become possible through confidence in him.

Now friends, this is exciting! And it is time we all become excited about it! Do you know why our kids yell and scream and cheer and cry and jump up and down at their high school ball games? They have a dream of winning the championship. The church has become too sophisticated to display much emotion today. But not so *after revival comes.* Sometimes we become a little emotional at First Baptist Church. We have been known to break into spontaneous applause during a baptismal service. Please don't repeat this, but we have on occasion even shouted a few "hallelujahs"! But you must understand: our walls are falling down and it's hard to keep quiet when you have a dream of winning the championship.

Well, the walls fell flat. How did the walls fall? Did the trumpet blast do it? Did the shout do it? Did the marching do it? As we look into the New Testament, we find in Hebrews 11:30 that, "By faith the walls of Jericho fell down, after they had been encircled for seven days." By faith! By faith! By faith! You see, the impossible becomes possible through confidence in God.

This is always the way God makes the impossible possible. We are living in a sense world. By that I mean we live by what we can see, hear, touch, taste, or smell. Faith is the process whereby we step out of the sense world and stand in the realm of the supernatural. By faith, the walls of Jericho fell flat. And by faith we can also overcome our obstacles. Those Israelites did not understand it all, but they walked. It seemed impossible, but they walked. It was totally against reason, but they walked. And God blessed their obedience and faith.

Where can we secure this faith? We receive it from the giver of all good things, God himself. Allow me, here and now, to dispel two of the devil's biggest lies concerning the faith life. One is, "I just don't have the faith." I say this kindly but firmly. That is a lie! The Scriptures tell us that "God has allotted to each a measure of faith" (Rom. 12:3). We have the faith. The real issue comes in where the object of our faith lies.

And in order to move faith into action, the object of our faith must be the Lord Jesus himself. Another blatant lie of the devil is, "I don't have *enough* faith." That, too, is a bald-faced lie! Jesus made it plain. It is not the quantity of our faith that matters. In fact, he said, "If you have faith as a mustard seed [small as that is] you shall say to this mountain, 'Move from here to there,' and it shall move" (Matt. 17:20). The faith life is the only life that is pleasing to God. "Without faith it is impossible to please [God]" (Heb. 11:6).

The key to opening the door of the faith life is found in Romans 10:17, "So faith comes from hearing, and hearing by the word of Christ." As you may already know, there is more than one Greek word in the New Testament that is translated by our English word for *word*. There is the *logos*. This is a word found, for example, in John, chapter 1. It is the written word.

But there is another little Greek word that is translated into the English *word*. It is the *rhema*. This is the personalized word that God gives to us in a certain situation. God takes a verse of Scripture and quickens it by his Spirit to our hearts. We realize it is just for us in that certain situation. A *rhema* is a specific word, to a specific person, in a specific situation. And this is where we find our faith! This is the word found in Romans 10:17, "Faith comes by hearing . . . and hearing by the word [rhema—the specific word] of Christ." The real problem with many of us in the faith life is that we have not been alone with God long enough to receive a word from him on which to stand. Joshua heard from God, and he stood on that word and his faith brought great victory!

I wonder how long we will keep trying to scale over our walls by human plans, schemes, techniques, and committees. God is not looking for new plans. He is looking for new persons. Jericho was taken because the warriors were not thinking about what they could do for God, but what God could do through them!

Here was a people, the children of Israel. They were in bondage, slaves of Pharaoh and Egypt. They came out of that bondage, through the Red Sea of salvation and into the wilderness wandering. Then they were at the banks of the Jordan, and they crossed through Jordan, turning their backs on an aimless life of wandering, and setting their feet in the Promised Land. But upon entering Canaan they were immediately confronted with a large obstacle—Jericho with its impregnable walls. What did they do? The unknown became known through communion. The unbelievable became believable through compliance. And the impossible became possible through confidence.

Here is a people, the fellowship of believers, giving the world a picture of the body of Christ in the 1980s. You and me! We were in bondage, slaves to sin and Satan. We've come through the Red Sea of salvation where some of us are still wandering in the wilderness. However, there are many who have crossed through Jordan and dwell in Canaan, only to find that there are walled cities and giants to conquer.

What shall we do? God is calling us to go on. God is spurring us to something supernatural. God is exhorting us to possess the land of Canaan, to overcome our obstacles. He has given us the land, but we can't possess it until the enemy is defeated. What shall we do? We will believe God, be obedient, and watch the unbelievable become believable. And we will put our trust and faith in God, and watch the impossible become possible before our very eyes.

God commanded the children of Israel to possess the land. He has commanded us to do exactly the same. In fact, he has made it plain in Ephesians 5:18, "Be filled with the Spirit." There are obstacles to overcome, walls of indifference, walls of unbelief, walls of pride, walls of broken relationships, and many others. But there is also a divine plan for overcoming these obstacles and living in victory.

Not long ago, Susie and I were having a few discipline problems with Wendy and Holly. The South Florida summer rains had isolated the girls in the house for several days. They became somewhat rowdy and irritable! It came to a head (or I would be more honest in saying a bottom) one particular night when Daddy had to do some rather firm disciplining.

I was in my office the next afternoon when the phone rang. Susie delightedly announced, "Wendy and Holly have been perfect angels all day." I quickly repeated a phrase I have used a thousand times—"I'll believe it when I see it!" And no more had those words escaped my lips until the truth came home to my heart.

That is our basic philosophy. It is no wonder our walls do not fall. It is no wonder our walls are such obstacles to us. It is no wonder so few of us are possessing the land. We are going through life saying, "I'll believe it when I see it!" We are no different from the scorner at the foot of the cross, shouting to Jesus, "Come on down from the cross, and *then* I'll believe you!" Our walls will fall when we begin to say, "I'll see it when I believe it!"

Friend, where are you right now? Are you at Jericho? Remember, Jericho is the place where we must decide whether we are going on with God or going to be content with a wilderness experience. You can overcome your obstacles.

God is calling us all to life on a higher plane. The unknown becomes known through communion. The unbelievable becomes believable through compliance. And the impossible becomes possible through confidence, *after revival comes.*

PRAYED INTO GOD'S FOREVER FAMILY

Gary had no time for God in his busy schedule. He was a handsome young businessman and doing quite well in his private enterprise. His life was governed by a consuming desire to achieve his goals at any cost. Consequently, he excused himself every Sunday morning when his wife, Kay, and the boys arose early and left for Sunday School and church. After all, it was the only morning he had to sleep and, to be quite truthful, he thought it would be somewhat hypocritical to use the "crutch" of a God he wasn't sure existed.

Gary became the prayer burden of a group of our young couples. They began to meet on Monday evenings to pray for his salvation and to enter the heavenlies, pulling down the strongholds of pride and priorities which bound him. And all the time Kay remained faithful, not only to God but to Gary.

On a particular Sunday morning, she returned from church to find her husband sitting in the middle of the bed. He was weeping uncontrollably. Now, men who are six feet six and full of pride normally don't make a habit of such activity. Kay quickly inquired, "What on earth has happened?" Gary sobbed, "I don't know. I am either having a nervous breakdown or I think I've just been saved!" Gary awoke that morning and something moved him to pick up the Bible Kay always left on her nightstand. He opened it to the Epistle of James

("Russian-Roulette" style) and began to read. Gary was saved in bed that morning. He was prayed into God's kingdom, and his wife had won him without a word.

Has it made a difference? Has it made a difference! He is walking, talking, living proof that "The effectual prayer of a righteous man can accomplish much" (Jas. 5:16). Incidently, people pray with power and get results "after revival comes."

Chapter 3
WHY ALL THIS MESS?

CHAPTER 3
Why All This Mess?
(Genesis 3:1-19)

I. Satan's Deceit Brings a Selfish Desire! (1-5)

"Now the serpent was more crafty than any beast of the field which the Lord God had made. And he said to the woman, 'Indeed, has God said, "You shall not eat from any tree of the garden?" ' " (v. 1).

"And the serpent said to the woman, 'You surely shall not die! "For God knows that in the day you eat from it your eyes will be opened, and you will be like God, knowing good and evil' " (vv. 4-5).

II. A Selfish Desire Brings a Sinful Decision! (6)

"When the woman saw that the tree was good for food, and that it was a delight to the eyes, and that the tree was desirable to make one wise, she took from its fruit and ate; and she gave also to her husband with her, and he ate" (v. 6).

III. A Sinful Decision Brings a Sure Defeat! (7-19)

A. Awareness of Self
"Then the eyes of both of them were opened, and they knew that they were naked" (v. 7).

B. Appearance of Shame
"and the man and his wife hid themselves from the presence of the Lord God among the trees of the garden" (v. 8).

56

C. Attitude of Sin

"And the man said, 'The woman whom Thou gavest to be with me, she gave me from the tree, and I ate.' "

"Then the Lord God said to the woman, 'What is this you have done?' And the woman said, 'The serpent deceived me, and I ate' " (vv. 12-13).

D. Anticipation of Separation

"To the woman He said, 'I will greatly multiply your pain in childbirth, In pain you shall bring forth children; Yet your desire shall be for your husband, and he shall rule over you' " (v. 16).

"By the sweat of your face You shall eat bread, Till you return to the ground, Because from it you were taken; For you are dust, And to dust you shall return" (v. 19).

Why All This Mess?

Now the serpent was more crafty than any beast of the field which the Lord God had made. And he said to the woman, "Indeed, has God said, 'You shall not eat from any tree of the garden'?"

And the woman said to the serpent, "From the fruit of the trees of the garden we may eat;

but from the fruit of the tree which is in the middle of the garden, God has said, 'You shall not eat from it or touch it, lest you die.' "

And the serpent said to the woman, "You surely shall not die!

"For God knows that in the day you eat from it your eyes will be opened, and you will be like God, knowing good and evil."

When the woman saw that the tree was good for food, and that it was a delight to the eyes, and that the tree was desirable to make one wise, she took from its fruit and ate; and she gave also to her husband with her, and he ate.

Then the eyes of both of them were opened, and they knew that they were naked; and they sewed fig leaves together and made themselves loin coverings.

And they heard the sound of the Lord God walking in the garden in the cool of the day, and the man and his wife hid themselves from the presence of the Lord God among the trees of the garden.

Then the Lord God called to the man, and said to him, "Where are you?"

And he said, "I heard the sound of Thee in the garden, and I was afraid because I was naked; so I hid myself."

And He said, "Who told you that you were naked? Have you eaten from the tree of which I commanded you not to eat?"

And the man said, "The woman whom Thou gavest to be with me, she gave me from the tree, and I ate."

Then the Lord God said to the woman, "What is this you have done?" And the woman said, "The serpent deceived me, and I ate."

And the Lord God said to the serpent,

"Because you have done this,
Cursed are you more than all
cattle,
And more than every beast of
the field:
On your belly shall you go,
And dust shall you eat
All the days of your life;
And I will put enmity
Between you and the woman,
And between your seed and
her seed;
He shall bruise you on the head,
And you shall bruise him on
the heel."

To the woman He said,
"I will greatly multiply
Your pain in childbirth,
In pain you shall bring forth
children;
Yet your desire shall be for
your husband,

And he shall rule over you."

Then to Adam He said, "Because you have listened to the voice of your wife, and have eaten from the tree about which I commanded you, saying, 'You shall not eat from it';

Cursed is the ground because
of you;
In toil you shall eat of it
All the days of your life.
"Both thorns and thistles it
shall grow for you;
And you shall eat the plants
of the field;
By the sweat of your face
You shall eat bread,
Till you return to the ground,
Because from it you were
taken;
For you are dust,
And to dust you shall return" (Gen. 3:1-19).

We live in an infected world. Each day, we awake to the front pages of our morning newspapers with headlines of violence and crime. During the writing of this chapter, I have noted the following headlines in our local newspaper:

GUNMAN GOES BERSERK—KILLS FIVE

MISSIONARY ASSASSINATED IN COLOMBIA

PROSTITUTES MAINTAIN HIGH PROFILE ON
CITY STREETS

THREE CHILDREN DIE AS AUTO
CAREENS OFF STREET: DRIVER
UNDER INFLUENCE

Yes, we are living in an infected world, a world infected with this disease of sin.

But why? Why all the wars? Why all the crime? Why all the murders? Why all the divorces? Why all the unrest and uncertainty? The answer can be directly traced to the fall of mankind recorded in Genesis 3. In fact, we see ourselves in these verses, struggling, groping for answers and asking, "Why?" The answer is found in exposing Satan's cunningly devised scheme that led to Adam and Eve's fall and is still his game plan for defeating us today.

For too long we have been putting the blame for the mess of our world on a montage of different opinions. Some shout that our mess results from Communist infiltration. Others claim inflation is driving people to crime. Still others contend it is the breakdown of the home. It is time we realize the root behind all these "fruits" of ruination. And, in a word, the root is the devil! Most churches are strangely silent about him and his activities today. Many have the idea, "I leave him alone, and he leaves me alone!" But the truth is if you have not met him head-on this week, you are going the same way he is going!

An army about to meet the enemy studies everything it can about enemy strategy and warfare. If we were a battalion of soldiers who were going into battle tomorrow, we would be heavily involved in preparation today. Our commander would gather us together and tell us everything he knew about the enemy. He would brief us on his strategy. He would tell us how he would attack and from which direction he would come. He would tell us what type of weapons our enemy would employ. And he would give us a battle plan for defeating our foe.

Strange, isn't it, when the church is engaged in a war how few leaders ever mention the enemy to the troops, much less instruct them about the battle. Is it any wonder so many Christians are defeated? It is hard to win a war if we do not know where or how it is being fought. This is precisely the focus of this chapter.

Satan's strategy is a series of cleverly designed steps which lead to our defeat and destruction. Simply stated, they are (1)

Satan's Deceit Brings a Selfish Desire, (2) A Selfish Desire Brings a Sinful Decision, and (3) A Sinful Decision Brings a Sure Defeat. Let's explore the devil and his deception in order to take positive action being victorious over him. We begin by noting:

SATAN'S DECEIT BRINGS A SELFISH DESIRE!
(Gen. 3:1-5)

Adam and Eve were the inhabitants of a perfect paradise. They lived in perfect harmony and perfect peace amid a perfect garden. The whole garden was theirs. They could eat of the fruits of the trees of the garden. Only of the tree of knowledge of good and evil in the middle of the garden had God forbidden them to eat. The world was theirs to have dominion over; the whole world—except for that one tree.

In this setting Satan came to tempt, deceive, and disrupt. He began by planting a tiny seed of doubt in Eve's mind. The devil may have asked, "Did God really mean that you could not eat from that tree? Would you really die if you ate of that tree? Come on now, Eve! Be realistic. God knows that as soon as you eat of that tree, you will become a god yourself, knowing good and evil." There he had planted a seed of doubt in Eve's heart and had given her a desire to eat of the tree of the knowledge of good and evil. He had pulled his first and most important ploy. Satan's deceit brings a selfish desire.

At this point, one might ask the question, "Why would God allow this disruption? If he has all power, why didn't he stop Satan?" Of course, this point could be belabored and debated from now on, but suffice it to say that, had God intervened then, our love to him would not be voluntary. We would be puppets instead of people. The love we voluntarily return to God is immeasurably priceless to him—so priceless that he allowed us to have the power of choice.

Now Satan had his foot in the door. He had sent a mist of doubt into Eve's mind and a selfish desire into her heart. James wrote that this is the game plan of the devil. "Each one is tempted when he is carried away and enticed by his own lust. Then when lust has conceived, it gives birth to sin; and when sin is accomplished, it brings forth death" (Jas. 1:14-15).

His attack is always the same whether he is inducing someone to live in adultery, to cheat on a business deal, or any number of other sinful activities. His strategy today is the same as it was with Eve in Eden's garden. He begins by creating a desire which leads to a decision which ultimately results in defeat.

Satan's strategy is simply to deposit that wrong desire in one's mind. The human mind is like a motel. The manager of a motel can't keep people in the lobby from asking for a room, but he can certainly keep them from getting one. It is the same with our thoughts. It is not a sin when a certain thought goes through our minds. The sin comes when we don't let it do just that—pass through our minds. Too often we give these satanic desires a room in our minds. This is when the devil gets his foot in the door. Remember, it is not a sin to be tempted. Our Lord was "tempted in all things as we are, yet without sin" (Heb. 4:15). The sin comes when we allow these thoughts to find harbor in our hearts.

Satan's deceit brings a selfish desire. It was true then as it is now. Satan is subtle and out to deceive us in any way that he can. Once he starts that evil desire stirring in our minds, over half his battle is already fought. He can step aside and watch that desire control our lives and become our master. Watch out! Selfish desire.

Let's move a step further in our quest for the answer to this *why?* by noticing that:

A SELFISH DESIRE BRINGS A SINFUL DECISION!
(Gen. 3:6)

A selfish desire brings a sinful decision. And what a sinful decision it was—they ate of the forbidden tree! After planting a selfish desire, the second step in Satan's chain of events is to bring about a sinful decision. Adam and Eve severed their perfect relationship with God by breaking his commandment. Remember, this act would not have taken place had the desire not preceded it.

Let's study exactly what happened. First, she looked at the tree and saw, "it was good for food." Second, she saw that it was a "delight to the eyes." Third, she saw that it was "desirable to make one wise" (v. 6).

Isn't this tactic the same one revealed to us in 1 John 2:16 concerning the three types of temptation? "For all that is in the world, the lust of the flesh and the lust of the eyes and the boastful pride of life, is not from the Father, but is from the world." There is the lust of the flesh—"It was good for food." There is the lust of the eyes—"It was a delight to the eyes." And there is the pride of life—it was "desirable to make one wise."

Wasn't this also Satan's strategy when he tempted Jesus in the wilderness? After Jesus had fasted forty days and forty nights, Satan began his temptation by saying, "If you are the Son of God, command that these stones become bread" (Matt. 4:3). Here is the "lust of the flesh," or as Eve said, "It was good for food." Satan also carried Jesus upon a high mountain so he could view the world as far as the eye could see. Then he said, "All these things will I give You, if You fall down and worship me" (Matt. 4:9). Here we view the "lust of the eyes," or as Eve said, "It was a delight to the eyes." Satan also ushered Jesus to the pinnacle of the Temple and said, "If You are the Son of God, throw Yourself down; for it is written, 'He will give His angels charge concerning you; and on their hands they will bear you up, lest you strike your foot against a stone' " (Matt. 4:6). Here was the "pride of life," or as Eve saw, "The tree was desirable to make one wise."

When we are tempted, it will be in one of these three areas—the lust of the flesh, the lust of the eyes, or the pride of life.

Are you beginning to recognize what is happening?

Satan's deception can be predictable! His strategy is becoming clear. He is reversing God's divine order of decision-making. God begins his dealing with us in the realm of the mind. There must be fact before there can be faith. For example, no person can be saved by faith in Jesus until that person knows the fact of Jesus' atoning death. In God's order, after the mind is exposed to the truth, the emotions will come into play. This gives rise to the decision to act and exercise faith in the fact that has been discovered.

Satan cleverly reverses this procedure. He makes his attack by appealing first to the emotions and will. For example, look at the advertising world. An attractive young lady enjoyably puffs on a certain brand of cigarette. In her sexy apparel, she acts as if it is the most exhilarating experience she has ever enjoyed. She is appealing to our desire and emotions, not to our minds. Our minds tell us smoking causes cancer, emphysema, and perhaps death. However, our desires tell us smoking is the "attractive" thing to do. This is Satan's strategy. He reverses the divine order of decision-making.

Once Satan had aroused the selfish desire in Eve, the sinful decision was almost certain to follow. I am amazed at how easy they fell. The Bible simply records, "She . . . ate and she gave also unto her husband with her, and he ate" (v. 6).

How true it is! A selfish desire brings a sinful decision. It was true then and it is true now. Warning! When Satan attacks, he will subtly plant an evil desire in your heart. All you have to do is let that desire lie around in your life, and it will overcome you. Like Adam and Eve, before you are aware, you will find yourself eating of the forbidden fruit. Remember, it all began with that selfish desire.

There is an insipid philosophy circulating in our culture today. Made popular by a famous comedian, the philosophy plainly stated is: "The devil made me do it!" In good English —baloney! The devil never made you do a thing. He merely put that desire in your heart, and you took it from there. There are many things being blamed on the devil today that are actually the result of the flesh. We will never overcome our enemy until we take personal responsibility for our actions.

The serpent did his wicked part, yes, but then bowed out of the scene. Eve took it from there! Our downfall always begins with that selfish desire.

There is a final step in this satanic strategy designed to defeat us.

A SINFUL DECISION BRINGS A SURE DEFEAT!
(Gen. 3:17-19)

After Adam and Eve rebelled against God, they were destined to die. As we come to this final step in Satan's cunning plan to defeat us, we are reminded that "when sin is accomplished, it brings forth death" (Jas. 1:15). There are a series of signs of this coming defeat listed in our text.

First of all, Adam and Eve developed an *awareness of self*. "Then the eyes of them both were opened, and they knew that they were naked; and they sewed fig leaves together and made themselves loin coverings" (v. 7). They saw that they were naked! It is intriguing that they had not noticed that until then. Until then God had been the center of their attention and devotion. They worshiped him supremely. But sin came and brought with it an awareness of self. Since that day everyone of us has had a problem with self. It is a sure sign of defeat when we allow ourselves to reign on the throne of our lives in the place of the Lord Jesus. It is a constant struggle but can be dealt with and put away.

Second, they developed an *appearance of shame*. "And they heard the sound of the Lord God walking in the garden in the cool of the day, And the man and his wife hid themselves from the presence of the Lord God among the trees of the garden" (v. 8). Because of their shame and guilt, they hid themselves from the presence of God. Until then, they had walked with God in the sweet fellowship of the garden. But sin brought with it an appearance of shame. Many today are hiding from God because of their guilt. It is a sign of defeat, egged on by the devil's deception.

The text reveals that "God [came walking] in the cool of the day." He was there to mend that broken relationship. He called, "Where are you, [Adam]?" Friend, God knew perfectly well where Adam was hiding. That was His way of getting Adam to see where Adam was!

Adam and Eve are prime examples of a third sign of the sure defeat that follows sinful decisions. They developed an *attitude of sin.* "And the man said, 'The woman whom Thou gavest to be with me, she gave me from the tree and I ate.' Then the Lord God said to the woman, 'What is this that you have done?' And the woman said, 'The serpent deceived me, and I ate' " (vv. 12-13).

They began to "pass the buck." Adam said, "Lord, she did it. She gave it to me!" Note that he even began to blame God. "The woman, *you gave me* . . . she did it," he cried as he pointed his finger at God with an attitude of sin. Then Eve said, "Lord, it was the serpent. He tempted me." Neither would accept responsibility for their actions. Aren't we just like that sometimes? Everyone is to blame but us! We are always innocent. It is always someone else's fault. When we remain in Adam, we will be characterized by an attitude of sin. It is a sure sign of defeat.

Finally, we see that Adam and Eve developed an *anticipation of separation* because of their sin. "To the woman He said, 'I will multiply your pain in childbirth, In pain you shall bring forth children; yet your desire shall be for your husband, and he shall rule over you' " (v. 16). To Adam he said, "By the sweat of your face you shall eat bread, Till you return to the ground; Because from it you were taken; For you are dust, And to dust you shall return" (v. 19). Pain, sweat, toil, and death were to characterize their lives and be their destinies. For thousands of years now, these strange creatures called men and women have appeared for a little while in a world of pain, sweat, toil, and death. They have lived their brief lives and their bodies have returned to the dust from which they came. A sinful decision brought, and still brings, a sure death. We begin to die the moment we are born and live our lives with an anticipation of separation to come. This is a sign of defeat.

We have now made it to the most exciting part of this chapter. Every word I have written thus far I have written to say: *there is an answer to this mess!* It is found, not in the first Adam, but in the second Adam, Jesus Christ. He is the One, the only One, who can remove us from our sins and place us in heavenly places. From the moment Eve put the fruit in her mouth and bit down, Jesus started getting ready to leave heaven for Bethlehem and Calvary. He gave his life that this might become a reality. He came to defeat the power of Satan and of death. He is our answer to the signs of defeat brought about by the deception of the devil.

What can Jesus do about our awareness of self? He has made provision. Listen to Galatians 2:20, "I have been crucified with Christ; and it is no longer I who live, but Christ lives in me; and the life which I now live in the flesh I live by faith in the Son of God who loved me, and delivered Himself up for me." He can put that old self to death. What can Jesus do about our appearance of shame? Listen to what happens to that person who commits his life to Jesus and finds the free pardon of sin He offers. "There is therefore now no condemnation for those who are in Christ Jesus . . . who do not walk according to the flesh, but according to the Spirit" (Rom. 8:1,4). No condemnation! What can Jesus do about our attitude of sin? Again, he has made provision. "If we confess our sins, He is faithful and righteous to forgive us our sins and to cleanse us from all unrighteousness" (1 John 1:9). What can Jesus do about the anticipation of separation which hovers over us? Here again, he has the answer. "Let not your heart be troubled; believe in God, believe also in Me. In My Father's house are many dwelling places; if it were not so, I would have told you; for I go to prepare a place for you. And if I go and prepare a place for you, I will come again, and receive you to Myself; that where I am, there ye may be also" (John 14:1-3).

Jesus Christ, the second Adam, comes to us amid our

messed-up, hustle-bustle, strife-filled world and offers to turn it into peace, patience, and joy. He is the one and only remedy to our selfish desires, our sinful decisions, and our sure defeats. He reverses the devil's activities and releases us from the devil's power when we admit our sins, accept his forgiveness, and commit ourselves to him as Lord and Master.

Why all this mess? Because Satan and his deceptive practices are as prevalent today as they were in Eden's garden. He is cunning and wise and leads us down a systematic pathway to destruction.

But this need not be our destiny. Satan can be defeated and his predictability can be exposed. We can combat him in the name of Jesus Christ and find freedom from his hold upon us. Just because he brings a selfish desire does not mean it has to result in a sinful decision.

It was a hot June day in Ada, Oklahoma. Early that morning I was pacing the second-floor corridor at Valley View Hospital. It was a special day for us. Holly was making her grand entrance into our world. It wasn't long until the doctor appeared at the nursery windows and held that little package of love in his arms. He laid her in a bassinet and wheeled her over near the window where I could get a good look. Only a daddy can know the joy of that moment. I stood there several minutes, thanking the Lord and watching that little red-faced beauty waving her arms and kicking her feet and crying at the top of her lungs.

Suddenly I noticed I was no longer standing there alone. A maid with her mop bucket was looking over my shoulder. "That your baby?" she asked. "Surely is," I proudly answered. She continued, "Well, it's no wonder she is crying. I mean being born into this kind of a world." And then she turned around and sauntered off down the hall, pushing her mop bucket before her. For a moment, I began to think, *You know, she is right. If I believe everything I preach and teach, then it would be far better for little Holly to go on to heaven right now. After all, she would not have to go through all the heart-aches of this life and would never have to have that haunting longing that only some moment of sin could be lived over again.*

I began to pray. It was an intimate moment, just Jesus and me and Holly. I pray stanzas of hymns often. That morning the Holy Spirit began to pray through me the words of a Bill Gaither hymn. When I began the second verse, I knew I was on holy ground.

> How sweet to hold a newborn baby,
> And feel the pride, and joy he gives;
> But greater still the calm assurance,
> This child can face uncertain days because
> he lives.
>
> Because he lives I can face tomorrow;
> Because he lives all fear is gone;
> Because I know he holds the future
> And life is worth the living just because
> he lives.*

There is victory in Jesus, *after revival comes!*

Learning to Love You, How Easy It Is!

Mario and I had absolutely nothing in common. Let's face it, an Italian cook and a young Baptist preacher don't usually "run" in the same circles. Before coming to Fort Lauderdale, I never would have dreamed that one of my best friends would be an Italian from New York. A Catholic Italian from New York, a Catholic Italian from New York who likes the opera, and what's more, a Catholic Italian from New York who likes the opera and cooks pizza and spaghetti for a living!

I am from Texas. We've always considered anything north of Wichita Falls Yankee territory. And the opera? Let's just say that it is not my favorite pastime.

What brings two people from such different backgrounds into an *agape* relationship? To begin with, pizza plays a part. I started stopping in his little Italian takeout restaurant for a slice of pizza a couple of nights a week. A relationship began to build, not around pizza but around the Lord Jesus. Jesus has been the center of a lot of intimate conversations at the back table of that little restaurant.

Mario and I together are taking some giant steps toward Jesus. He is like thousands of others in my city, and yours, working hard, minding his business, and waiting, just waiting for someone to say over a piece of pizza, "Jesus really loves you and so do I."

We are learning that prejudices and differing backgrounds melt away under the warmth of *agape* love . . . *after revival comes.*

Chapter 4
GIANTS: PROBLEMS OR POSSIBILITIES?

CHAPTER 4
Giants: Problems or Possibilities?
(1 Samuel 17:1-54)

I. Step 1: Properly Evaluate the Situation (1-30)

    A. A Problem
"Now the Philistines gathered their armies for battle; . . .
And Saul and the men of Israel were gathered, and camped
in the valley of Elah" (vv. 1-2).
"Then a champion came out from the armies of the Philistines named Goliath, from Gath, whose height was six
cubits and a span" (v. 4).
"Saul and all Israel . . . were dismayed and greatly afraid"
(v. 11).
"And the Philistine came forward morning and evening for
forty days, and took his stand" (v. 16).

    B. A Possibility
"Then David spoke to the men who were standing by him,
saying, 'What will be done for the man who kills this Philistine, and takes away the reproach from Israel? For who is
this uncircumcised Philistine, that he should taunt the
armies of the living God?' " (v. 26).

II. Step 2: Persistently Employ the Solution (31-47)

    A. An Unqualified Faith
"And David said to Saul, 'Let no man's heart fail on account
of him; your servant will go and fight with this Philistine' "
(v. 32).

"And David said, 'The Lord who delivered me from the paw of the lion and from the paw of the bear, He will deliver me from the hand of this Philistine' " (v. 37).

B. An Uncompromising Faith
"Then Saul clothed David with his garments and put a bronze helmet on his head, and he clothed him with armor.
"David said to Saul, 'I cannot go with these. . . . And David took them off.
"And he took . . . five smooth stones from the brook, and put them in the shepherd's bag which he had, even in his pouch, and his sling was in his hand; and he approached the Philistine" (vv. 38,39b-40).

C. An Unselfish Faith
"Then David said to the Philistine, 'You come to me with a sword, a spear, and a javelin, but I come to you in the name of the Lord.
'This day the Lord will deliver you up into my hands.
for the battle is the Lord's and He will give you into our hands' " (vv. 45a,46a,47b).

III. Step 3: Personally Enjoy the Spoils (48-54)

A. The Victory
"And David . . . took . . . a stone and slung it, and struck the Philistine on his forehead.
"Thus David prevailed over the Philistine with a sling and a stone (vv. 49a,50a).

B. The Victor
"Then David took the Philistine's head and brought it to Jerusalem" (v. 54).

Giants: Problems or Possibilities?

Now the Philistines gathered their armies for battle; and they were gathered at Socoh which belongs to Judah, and they camped between Socoh and Azekah, in Ephesdammim.

And Saul and the men of Israel were gathered, and camped in the valley of Elah, and drew up in battle array to encounter the Philistines.

And the Philistines stood on the mountain on one side while Israel stood on the mountain on the other side, with the valley between them.

Then a champion came out from the armies of the Philistines named Goliath, from Gath, whose height was six cubits and a span.

And he had a bronze helmet on his head, and he was clothed with scale armor which weighed five thousand shekels of bronze.

He also had bronze greaves on his legs and a bronze javelin slung between his shoulders.

And the shaft of his spear was like a weaver's beam, and the head of his spear weighed six hundred shekels of iron; his shield-carrier also walked before him.

And he stood and shouted to the ranks of Israel, and said to them, "Why do you come out to draw up in battle array? Am I not the Philistine and you servants of Saul? Choose a man for yourselves and let him come down to me.

"If he is able to fight with me and kill me, then we will become your servants; but if I prevail against him and kill him, then you shall become our servants and serve us."

Again the Philistine said, "I defy the ranks of Israel this day; give me a man that we may fight together."

When Saul and all Israel heard these words of the Philistine, they were dismayed and greatly afraid.

Now David was the son of the Ephrathite of Bethlehem in Judah, whose name was Jesse, and he had eight sons. And Jesse was old in the days of Saul, advanced in years among men.

And the three older sons of Jesse had gone after Saul to the battle. And the names of his three sons who went to the battle were Eliab the first-born, and the second to him Abinadab, and the third Shammah.

And David was the youngest. Now the three oldest followed Saul,

but David went back and forth from Saul to tend his father's flock at Bethlehem.

And the Philistine came forward morning and evening for forty days, and took his stand.

Then Jesse said to David his son, "Take now for your brothers an ephah of this roasted grain and these ten loaves, and run to the camp to your brothers.

"Bring also these ten cuts of cheese to the commander of their thousand, and look into the welfare of your brothers, and bring back news of them.

"For Saul and they and all the men of Israel are in the valley of Elah, fighting with the Philistines."

So David arose early in the morning and left the flock with a keeper and took the supplies and went as Jesse had commanded him. And he came to the circle of the camp while the army was going out in battle array shouting the war cry.

And Israel and the Philistines drew up in battle array, army against army.

Then David left his baggage in the care of the baggage keeper, and ran to the battle line and entered in order to greet his brothers.

As he was talking with them, behold, the champion,

the Philistine from Gath named Goliath, was coming up from the army of the Philistines, and he spoke these same words; and David heard them.

When all the men of Israel saw the man, they fled from him and were greatly afraid.

And the men of Israel said, "Have you seen this man who is coming up? Surely he is coming up to defy Israel. And it will be that the king will enrich the man who kills him with great riches and will give him his daughter and make his father's house free in Israel."

Then David spoke to the men who were standing by him, saying, "What will be done for the man who kills this Philistine, and takes away the reproach from Israel? For who is this uncircumcised Philistine, that he should taunt the armies of the living God?"

And the people answered him in accord with this word, saying, "Thus it will be done for the man who kills him."

Now Eliab his oldest brother heard when he spoke to the men; and Eliab's anger burned against David and he said, "Why have you come down? And with whom have you left those few sheep in the wilderness? I know your insolence and the wickedness of your heart; for you have come down in order to see the battle."

But David said, "What have I done now? Was it not just a question?"

Then he turned away from him to another and said the same thing; and the people answered the same thing as before.

When the words which David spoke were heard, they told them to Saul, and he sent for him.

And David said to Saul, "Let no man's heart fail on account of him; your servant will go and fight with this Philistine."

Then Saul said to David, "You are not able to go against this Philistine to fight with him; for you are but a youth while he has been a warrior from his youth."

But David said to Saul, "Your servant was tending his father's sheep. When a lion or a bear came and took a lamb from the flock,

"I went out after him and attacked him and rescued it

from his mouth; and when he rose up against me, I seized him by his beard and struck him and killed him.

"Your servant has killed both the lion and the bear; and this uncircumcised Philistine will be like one of them, since he has taunted the armies of the living God."

And David said, "The Lord who delivered me from the paw of the lion and from the paw of the bear, He will deliver me from the hand of this Philistine." And Saul said to David, "Go, and may the Lord be with you."

Then Saul clothed David with his garments and put a bronze helmet on his head, and he clothed him with armor.

And David girded his sword over his armor and tried to walk, for he had not tested them. So David said to Saul, "I cannot go with these, for I have not tested them." And David took them off.

And he took his stick in his hand and chose for himself five smooth stones from the brook, and put them in the shepherd's bag which he had, even in his pouch, and his sling was in his hand; and he approached the Philistine.

Then the Philistine came on and approached David, with the shield-bearer in front of him.

When the Philistine looked and saw David, he disdained him; for he was but a youth, and ruddy, with a handsome appearance.

And the Philistine said to David, "Am I a dog, that you come to me with sticks?" And the Philistine cursed David by his gods.

The Philistine also said to David, "Come to me and I will give your flesh to the birds of the sky and the beasts of the field."

Then David said to the Philistine, "You come to me with a sword, a spear, and a javelin, but I come to you in the name of the Lord of hosts, the God of the armies of Israel, whom you have taunted.

"This day the Lord will deliver you up into my hands, and I will strike you down and remove your head from you. And I will give the dead bodies of the army of the Philistines this day to the birds of the sky and the wild beasts of the earth, that all the earth may know that there is a God in Israel, "and that all this assembly may know that the Lord does not deliver by sword or by spear; for the battle is the Lord's and He will give you into our hands."

Then it happened when the Philistine rose and came and drew near to meet David, that David ran quickly toward the battle line to meet the Philistine.

And David put his hand into his bag and took from it a stone and slung it, and struck the Philistine on his forehead. And the stone sank into his forehead, so that he fell on his face to the ground.

Thus David prevailed over the Philistine with a sling and a stone, and he struck the Philistine and killed him; but there was no sword in David's hand.

Then David ran and stood over the Philistine and took his sword and drew it out of its sheath and killed him, and cut off his head with it. When the Philistines saw that their champion was dead, they fled.

And the men of Israel and Judah arose and shouted and pursued the Philistines as far as the entrance to the valley, and to the gates of Ekron. And the slain Philistines lay along the way to Shaaraim, even to Gath and Ekron.

And the sons of Israel returned from chasing the Philistines and plundered their camps.

Then David took the Philistine's head and brought it to Jerusalem, but he put his weapons in his tent (1 Sam. 17:1-54).

One of the most familiar stories in the Bible involves David and Goliath and the confrontation between the armies of Israel and the Philistines. We all know the story well. The Philistines stood on one mountain and the Israelites on another with the valley of Elah in between.

The champion of the armies of the Philistines stepped out and made a challenge. He offered to fight against any one of the Israelites and the loser's people would become the servants of the winner. That Philistine was quite a man. His name was Goliath and he stood over nine feet tall. Needless to say, there were no volunteers from the Israelite camp. In fact, the Bible records that "When Saul and all Israel heard these words of the Philistine, they were dismayed and greatly afraid" (1 Sam. 17:11).

Into this setting appeared the shepherd boy, David, delivering supplies from home to his three older brothers. Upon arriving in the camp, he heard the taunting of this giant across the valley and became appalled at the cowardice of the armies of the living God and the giant's ridicule of God's people. Now, we are familiar with the rest of the story: David, with his sling, slew the giant and won a great victory for God!

Here we see a tremendous scriptural truth unfolding. Even though Saul was still on the throne, David had just been anointed future king over Israel (1 Sam. 16). Immediately he was confronted with a giant of a problem. In almost very book of the Bible this truth is revealed. In the Book of Joshua, immediately after entering the Promised Land, the Israelites were confronted with the walls of Jericho. In 1 Kings, on the heels of the resounding victory on Mount Carmel, Elijah was confronted with angry King Ahab. In Nehemiah, as soon as they began to rebuild the broken walls, they were opposed by Sanballat, Tobiah, and the others.

In the life of David, right after being anointed king by Samuel, he was confronted with the giant, Goliath. We must grasp this scriptural truth: When God does a work, we must expect the devil to raise his ugly head in opposition. Goliath is a picture of the devil, seeking to terrify and bring into captivity those who bear the name of the Lord. He always rises up when God is doing a work. Paul reminds us that "all who desire to live godly in Christ Jesus will be persecuted" (2 Tim. 3:12).

Even though the story of David and Goliath is so familiar, I fear that often many have missed its deepest spiritual significance, for it really deals with what to do when giants confront us. Perhaps you are confronted with a giant right now. What about your giant? Is it a problem to you or a possibility for you? For the Spirit-filled believer, we are about to recognize that when our giant flexes his muscles, we can turn him into limitless possibilities to glorify God! How can we defeat these giants of life? What are we to do when a giant confronts us? Let's begin by observing:

Step 1: Properly Evaluate the Situation
(1 Sam. 17:1-30)

It is quite obvious that the Israelites were faced with a difficult situation. The giant had become their problem. Twice a day for forty days, he strutted up and down one side of the valley, mocking and taunting the Israelites. In all his strength and stature he seemed absolutely beyond defeat. Forty days! This is always the period in Scripture which is associated with testing. Moses spent forty years on the backside of the desert. Joshua and Caleb lived forty years wandering in the wilderness with Canaan in their hearts. Jesus was tempted of the devil forty days in the wilderness. The more Goliath taunted, the more cowardly and pathetic became the situation in the Israelite camp. The Bible records, "When all the men of Israel saw the man, they fled from him and were greatly afraid" (1 Sam. 17:24).

Then came David! How differently he evaluated the situation. He looked upon Goliath, not as a problem, but as a possibility to glorify God. He could not understand the apathy and fear in the hearts of the people of God. He sized up the giant and saw the possibility of a miracle. He knew that was what it would take. But after all, our Lord Jesus never performed a miracle that did not begin at the platform of a problem. He fed five thousand people. Why? Because they were hungry. He healed a man who had not walked in thirty-eight years. Why? Because he was lame. He gave sight to the blind. Why? Because they could not see. If we are ever to learn how to defeat our giant, we must first learn to properly evaluate the situation.

It will do us well to understand what a problem really is! Definition: A problem is the platform upon which God desires to show how wonderfully he can provide. I once heard Tom Eliff define a problem as "an indication from God that he has a blessing for you . . . which you've been too blind to ask him for. Consequently, a situation comes into your life in order to get you to the place where you will ask God for what he's been wanting to give you all along." Every problem we have has been seen by God before it reaches us. Did it ever occur to you that God never allows anything to reach you that he does not intend to turn to your good? "And we know that God causes all things to work together for good to those who love God, to those who are called according to His purpose" (Rom. 8:28).

Most of us confront our problems and say, "Oh no, I knew that was going to happen! I was afraid of that!" That is our first mistake. Look at Job! Remember how he acted before he lost his family, his friends, his health, and his wealth? He worried and fretted about losing them. How do we know this? Because when he finally lost his family, his friends, his health, and his wealth, the first thing he said was, "For what I fear comes upon me" (Job 3:25). Our first reaction to a giant is usually, "Oh no, I was afraid of that!"

Instead, when a problem knocks at our door, we should step up boldly, open the door, invite it in, put on the coffee, sit it down in our parlor, and say, "I'm glad you're here! You're a reminder to me that God has a blessing for me for which I've been too blind to ask him. So he sent you here in order for me to come to the point of trusting him—so he could give me what he has wanted to give me all along!"

How do you view your giants? Are they problems or possibilities? The Israelites stared at the giant and saw a problem. For forty days they focused all their attention on the giant, and he became a problem. Fear, doubt, and defeat set in.

On the other hand, David looked at that giant and saw nothing but possibility and ultimate blessing. He didn't focus his attention on the giant, but on the living God. The result was joy and faith and victory!

Now, what about that giant in your life? If you focus all your attention on him, he will become a problem. Fear, doubt, and defeat will be your destiny. But, if like David, you recognize him as an opportunity for God to work a miracle and keep your eyes on Jesus, joy, faith, and victory can be the result.

The giant is truly not the problem. The real problem is your evaluation of him. If we are ever to overcome the giants of life, we must first of all properly evaluate them. The giant is God's means of getting us to ask Him for the blessing He has been waiting to give us all along! Properly evaluate the situation. The giant is not a problem, but a possibility! That giant in your life (whatever or whoever it might be) is an opportunity for God to work a miracle!

Once we have properly evaluated our situation, then we come to:

Step 2: Persistently Employ the Solution
(1 Sam. 17:31-47)

What is the solution to defeating the Goliaths of life? It's found in the text. Let's look and learn together from these exciting verses. First of all, David exhibited an *unqualified faith!*

"When the words which David spoke were heard, they told them to Saul, and he sent for him. And David said to Saul, 'Let no man's heart fail on account of him; your servant will go and fight with this Philistine.' Then Saul said to David, 'You are not able to go against this Philistine to fight with him; for you are but a youth while he has been a warrior from his youth.' But David said to Saul, 'Your servant was tending his father's sheep. When a lion or a bear came and took a lamb from the flock, I went out after him and attacked him, and rescued it from his mouth; and when he rose up against me, I seized him by his beard and struck him and killed him. Your servant has killed both the lion and the bear; and this uncircumcised Philistine will be like one of them, since he has taunted the armies of the living God.' And David said, 'The Lord who delivered me from the paw of the lion and from the paw of the bear, He will deliver me from the hand of this Philistine.' And Saul said to David, 'Go, and may the Lord be with you' " (1 Sam. 17:31-37).

In verse 37 he said, "The Lord who delivered me from the paw of the lion and from the paw of the bear, He will deliver me from the hand of this Philistine." He didn't say, "He can deliver me from the hand of the Philistine." David said, "He *will* deliver me from the hand of this Philistine."

It was alone in the shepherd's field that David learned to live by faith. There around Bethlehem he made preparation to meet Goliath in the valley of Elah. There he killed the bear and the lion by faith. This is usually the way God teaches the principle of faith to godly people—that is, alone in some shepherd field. For example, Elijah didn't learn about faith on Mount Carmel. He learned the principles of faith alone at the brook Cherith and at the widow's home in Zarephath!

David had an unqualified faith. There was no doubt in his mind, and there was no fear in his heart. Doubt and fear cannot reside in the life of a Spirit-filled believer! Faith and faith alone is the victory. Faith does not bring victory. Faith *is* the victory! It may be that before the giant in your life is ever really defeated, you will have to find yourself alone in a shepherd's field, doing business with God, learning to live with an unqualified faith in the living God.

David also had an *uncompromising faith!*

"Then Saul clothed David with his garments and put a bronze helmet on his head, and he clothed him with armor. And David girded his sword over his armor and tried to walk, for he had not tested them. So David said to Saul, 'I cannot go with these, for I have not tested them.' And David took them off. And he took his stick in his hand and chose for himself five smooth stones from the brook, and put them in the shepherd's bag which he had, even in his pouch, and his sling was in his hand; and he approached the Philistine" (1 Sam. 17:38-40).

Saul wanted David to fight the battle in his own armor. Saul wanted to dress David up as much like Goliath as possible. But David knew that the victory was "not by might nor by power, but by [God's] Spirit" (Zech. 4:6).

Too many of us feel that the best way to overcome our giants is to utilize the world's methods. We try to solve our problems by the world's standards. Why? Because we don't properly evaluate our situation and recognize our giants for what they really are. David took off Saul's armor and took what he had, a simple slingshot, into battle. You see, Saul's armor will not do! We must use what God supplies (smooth stones of faith) instead of what man offers! Too many of us have gone out to meet our giants and have come back battered and beaten because we thought worldly methods were sufficient.

Then again, David also exhibited an *unselfish faith!*

> "Then the Philistine came on and approached David, with the shield-bearer in front of him. When the Philistine looked and saw David, he disdained him; for he was but a youth, and ruddy, with a handsome appearance. And the Philistine said to David, 'Am I a dog, that you come to me with sticks?' And the Philistine cursed David by his gods. The Philistine also said to David, 'Come to me, and I will give your flesh to the birds of the sky and the beasts of the field.' Then David said to the Philistine, 'You come to me with a sword, a spear, and a javelin, but I come to you in the name of the Lord of hosts, the God of the armies of Israel, whom you have taunted. This day the Lord will deliver you up into my hands, and I will strike you down and remove your head from you. And I will give the dead bodies of the army of the Philistines this day to the birds of the sky and the wild beasts of the earth, that all the earth may know that the Lord does not deliver by sword or by spear; for the battle is the Lord's and He will give you into our hands' " (1 Sam. 17:41-47).

David said, "You come to me with a sword, . . . but I come to you in the name of the Lord of hosts . . . for the battle is the Lord's" (vv. 45-47). David acknowledged that the battle was the Lord's! He sought no personal glory for himself. When you live by faith, you'd better have "self" out of the way! The man who walks by faith will not be popular among carnal men. Look at David! When he began to walk by faith, he was taunted by his own brother, Eliab.

"Now Eliab his oldest brother heard when he spoke to the men; and Eliab's anger burned against David and he said, 'Why have you come down? And with whom have you left those few sheep in the wilderness? I know your insolence and the wickedness of your heart; for you have come down in order to see the battle' " (1 Sam. 17:28).

Not only was he taunted by Eliab, but he was discouraged by Saul. "Then Saul said to David,

'You are not able to go against this Philistine to fight with him; for you are but a youth while he has been a warrior from his youth' " (1 Sam. 17:33). And finally, after being taunted by his own brother and discouraged by his own king, he was scorned by Goliath. "When the Philistine looked and saw David, he disdained him; for he was but a youth, and ruddy, with a handsome appearance. And the Philistine said to David, 'Am I a dog, that you come to me with sticks?' And the Philistine cursed David by his gods. The Philistine also said to David, 'Come to me, and I will give your flesh to the birds of the sky and the beasts of the field' " (1 Sam. 17:42-44).

The key to the solution is found in verse 47: "For the battle is the Lord's!" You see, God wants to fight your battle and kill your giant for you. David didn't kill Goliath! God did! David was merely able to be an instrument through an unqualified faith, an uncompromising faith, and an unselfish faith. Faith is the victory!

So, you have a giant that needs killing? Oh, I see, you have been focusing all your attention on him! What is that? Oh yes, fear has set in. And doubt! Oh, you have been wear-

ing Saul's armor, using worldly methods to overcome him.
What is that? Oh, I see. The giant is still there! Listen, the
battle is the Lord's! Faith is the victory! It is by faith, by faith,
by faith! Believe that God is allowing that giant to remain
because He has a blessing for you which He has been wanting
to give you all along!

All Israel had their eyes on Goliath. If David had not
come along when he did, they would still be faced with their
giant. He never would have left them, until he and his cohorts
killed them!

If we are to overcome the giants of this life, we must not
just properly evaluate our situation, but we must persistently
employ the solution, and that is, faith! When common sense
dictated that the situation was hopeless David appeared on
the scene, and he had the uncommon sense to believe God
could make the impossible possible, and he slew the giant
Goliath by faith! This is a challenge for us to believe what we
can't always see. Not to say, "I will believe it when I see it,"
but instead, "I will see it when I believe it!"

There is a final step in destroying the giants of this life.
We come finally to:

Step 3: Personally Enjoy the Spoils
(1 Sam. 17:48-54)

The story is so familiar, it scarcely needs repeating. David
slew the giant, Goliath, in the valley of Elah with one shot
from his sling. Goliath was no problem to the man of God
who had his eyes fixed on the Lord and lived by faith!

And do you know something? Your Goliath will cease to
be a problem, and you can personally enjoy the spoils of victory, if you will fix your eyes on Jesus and live by faith. Faith
had won the day! With faith, all things are possible (cf. Luke
1:37).

Note verses 51-54: "Then David ran and stood over the
Philistine and took his sword and drew it out of its sheath and
killed him, and cut off his head with it. When the Philistines

saw that their champion was dead, they fled" (1 Sam. 17:51). "Then David took the Philistine's head and brought it to Jerusalem, but he put his weapons in his tent" (1 Sam. 17:54).

Can you picture it? There was little David. Faith had triumphed. Now he stood on the chest of that giant and chopped off his head. He was personally enjoying the spoils of victory. What rejoicing took place in Jerusalem when they returned home with the spoils of war!

I wonder how many people reading these words would like to chop the head off of their giant and personally enjoy the spoils of victory? Remember, the giant is really not in the way to victory, you are! The battle is the Lord's. The victory is the Lord's. Faith is the victory. Stand in it. Receive it!

There is an interesting by-product in verse 52! "And the men of Israel and Judah arose and shouted and pursued the Philistines as far as the entrance to the valley, and to the gates of Ekron. And the slain Philistines lay along the way to Shaaraim, even to Gath and Ekron" (1 Sam. 17:52).

When we live by faith, we encourage others. Every Israelite became a victor that day because of David's triumph. They all shared in the victory! Friend, Jesus has won the victory, already, two thousand years ago! We can share in that total victory today, by faith.

God is not only a God of things past or things to come! He is a God of the now! He is Lord today. Too many of us think of God simply as a great historic figure of the Old or the New Testaments—that great God of the past who performed many wonders, works, and miracles in the Word of God. Others thinking of God look only to the God of the future and our blessed hope, that is, "the glorious appearing" of our Lord and Savior, Jesus Christ, and the God of the second coming and the God of heaven. But the most exciting thought to my heart is that Jesus is alive today. He is the God of the now! And he is extremely interested in the giants in your life. It is a sad commentary, but the "now God" of most of us is too small to be the God of the Bible!

In Saul's mind, God was absent from the whole conflict.

He had no part whatsoever in it. This is how it is with many people today. A giant comes along and some people, even Christians, act as if God were absent from the whole conflict. What a tragedy!

But note the difference in David. In David's mind, the Lord was the most glorious reality of all! He saw that giant as a possibility, not as a problem. He put his faith in the living God and acknowledged that the Lord would deliver him— because he came in the name of the Lord, and after all the battle was the Lord's. Let me ask you—is Jesus real to you today? Do you understand that the battle is the Lord's? Oh, how he longs to turn your problem into a possibility of "joy unspeakable and full of glory"!

So, you have a giant? So you want to defeat him? Here's how: Begin by *properly evaluating the situation*. That giant is not a problem. He is a possibility to glorify God and receive a blessing from God. Remember, Jesus never performed a miracle that did not begin at the platform of a problem. Then after properly evaluating the situation, *persistently employ the solution*. Remember, faith *is* the victory. And once you have done these two, go ahead and *personally enjoy the spoils!* Believe where you can't see. Stand erect on the chest of your giant and chop his head off, by faith.

What is your giant, a problem or a possibility? He is always a possibility, *after revival comes*.

Passing the Cup

Fort Lauderdale has the dubious distinction of being one of the few cities in the world where there are more automobiles registered than there are people who live here! Having well over one million automobiles on file sounds great when the Chamber of Commerce tries to promote our affluence and prosperity, but it is quite another matter when the time comes each year to have your automobile inspected. Lines! Lines! Lines! It is not uncommon to wait four to five hours in lines that are several blocks long!

Well, judgment comes sooner or later, and it caught up with me again some time back. Knowing that the inspection station opened at 8:00 AM, I decided to beat the crowd by arriving two hours early, prepared to spend time in study while I waited in line. Arriving in the darkness, I was delighted to see there were *only forty-three* cars ahead of me.

As the sun came up, I began to read my Bible. After what seemed like a few weeks, I found myself entering the pavilion and approaching the "assembly lines" which checked my headlights, brakes, windshield wipers, and so on. As I drove through the line, the young man who checked the wiper blades came to the window.

"Is that a Bible lying on your front seat?" he asked. "Yes,"

91

I replied, "Have you ever read one?" He answered, "No, but I'm thinking about starting."

He then remarked, "You must be a Baptist!" "Yes," I proudly replied. He then said, "I'll bet you go to that big Baptist church downtown." "Yes, I do!" I answered and added, "But why would you say that?" "Because almost daily someone from that church drives through with a smile and a warm invitation to church. Some have even told me what Jesus has done in their lives!"

After revival comes, it begins to affect the atmosphere of the whole area. People, who for years have sat silently, suddenly "cannot stop speaking what we have seen and heard" (Acts 4:20), even in the normal traffic patterns of life. People who have tasted of living water can't help but pass the cup, *after revival comes!*

Chapter 5
SOS: SOLVING OUR SETBACKS

CHAPTER 5
SOS: Solving Our Setbacks
(Joshua 7:1-21)

I.   Acknowledge the Source of Our Setbacks (1-3)

    A. Self-Reliance
"But the sons of Israel acted unfaithfully in regard to the things under the ban, for Achan, . . . took some of the things under the ban, . . . Now Joshua sent men from Jericho to Ai, . . ."Go up and spy out the land.' So the men went up and spied out Ai," (vv. 1*a*,2).

    B. Self-Confidence
"Do not let all the people go up; only about two or three thousand men need go up to Ai; do not make all the people toil up there, for they are few" (v. 3).

    C. Self-Centeredness
"But the sons of Israel acted unfaithfully in regard to the things under the ban, for Achan, . . . took some of the things under the ban" (v. 1)

II. Ascertain the Side Effects of Our Setbacks (4-9)

    A. Brings Defeat
"So about three thousand men from the people went up there, but they fled from the men of Ai.
And the men of Ai struck down about thirty-six of their men, . . . the hearts of the people melted and became as water" (vv. 4-5*a*).

94

B. Brings Discouragement

"And Joshua said, 'Alas, O Lord God, why didst Thou ever bring this people over the Jordan, only to deliver us into the hand of the Amorites, to destroy us? If only we had been willing to dwell beyond the Jordan!' " (v. 7).

C. Brings Doubt

"Oh Lord, what can I say since Israel has turned their back before their enemies?

"For the Canaanites and all the inhabitants of the land will hear of it, and they will surround us and cut off our name from the earth" (vv. 8-9a).

D. Brings Dishonor

"And what wilt Thou do for Thy great name?" (v.9b).

III. Apply the Solution to Our Setbacks (10-21)

A. Conviction

"So the Lord said to Joshua, 'Rise up!

Israel has sinned

I will not be with you any more unless you destroy the things under the ban from your midst' " (v. 10a,11a,12b).

B. Consecration

"Rise up! Consecrate the people and say, 'Consecrate yourselves' "(v. 13).

C. Compliance

"So Joshua arose early in the morning and brought Israel near by tribes, and the tribe of Judah was taken" (v. 16).

D. Confession

"So Achan answered Joshua and said, 'Truly, I have sinned against the Lord, . . .

when I saw . . . then I coveted . . . and took . . . and . . . concealed' " (vv. 20-21).

SOS: Solving Our Setbacks

But the sons of Israel acted unfaithfully in regard to the things under the ban, for Achan, the son of Carmi, the son of Zabdi, the son of Zerah, from the tribe of Judah, took some of the things under the ban, therefore the anger of the Lord burned against the sons of Israel.

Now Joshua sent men from Jericho to Ai, which is near Bethaven, east of Bethel, and said to them, "Go up and spy out the land." So the men went up and spied out Ai.

And they returned to Joshua and said to him, "Do not let all the people go up; only about two or three thousand men need go up to Ai; do not make all the people toil up there, for they are few."

So about three thousand men from the people went up there, but they fled from the men of Ai.

And the men of Ai struck down about thirty-six of their men, and pursued them from the gate as far as Shebarim, and struck them down on the descent, so the hearts of the people melted and became as water.

Then Joshua tore his clothes and fell to the earth on his face before the ark of the Lord until the evening, both he and the elders of Israel; and they put dust on their heads.

And Joshua said, "Alas, O Lord God, why didst Thou ever bring this people over the Jordan, only to deliver us into the hand of the Amorites, to destroy us? If only we had been willing to dwell beyond the Jordan!

"Oh Lord, what can I say since Israel has turned their back before their enemies?

"For the Canaanites and all the inhabitants of the land will hear of it, and they will surround us and cut off our name from the earth. And what wilt Thou do for Thy great name?"

So the Lord said to Joshua, "Rise up! Why is it that you have fallen on your face?

"Israel has sinned, and they have also transgressed My covenant which I commanded them. And they have even taken some of the things under the ban and have both stolen and deceived. Moreover, they have also put them among their own things.

"Therefore the sons of Israel cannot stand before their enemies; they turn their backs before their enemies, for they have become accursed. I will not be with you any more unless you destroy the things under the ban from your midst.

"Rise up! Consecrate the people and say, 'Consecrate yourselves for tomorrow, for thus the Lord, the God of Israel, has said, "There are things under the ban in your midst, O Israel. You cannot stand before your enemies until you have removed the things under the ban from your midst."

'In the morning you shall come near by your tribes. And it shall be that the tribe which the Lord takes by lot shall come near by families, and the family which the Lord takes shall come near by households, and the household which the Lord takes shall come near man by man.

'And it shall be that the one who is taken with the things under the ban shall be burned with fire, he and all that belongs to him, because he has transgressed the covenant of the Lord, and because he has committed a disgraceful thing in Israel.' "

So Joshua arose early in the morning and brought Israel near by tribes, and the tribe of Judah was taken.

And he brought the family of Judah near, and he took the family of the Zerahites; and he brought the family of the Zerahites near man by man, and Zabdi was taken.

And he brought his household near man by man; and
Achan, son of Carmi, son of Zabdi, son of Zerah, from the
tribe of Judah was taken.

Then Joshua said to Achan, "My son, I implore you,
give glory to the Lord, the God of Israel, and give praise to
Him; and tell me now what you have done. Do not hide it
from me."

So Achan answered Joshua and said, "Truly, I have
sinned against the Lord, the God of Israel, and this is what I
did; When I saw among the spoil a beautiful mantle from
Shinar and two hundred shekels of silver and a bar of gold
fifty shekels in weight, then I coveted them and took them;
and behold, they are concealed in the earth inside my tent
with the silver underneath it" (Josh. 7:1-21).

The story unfolds late one night in the Israelite camp.
The Israelites had just won the victory at Jericho and all the
camp was asleep. All, that is, but one—Achan! He stood at
the entrance to his tent, looking first one way and then the
other. Then, cautiously, quietly, and stooping very low
through the shadows, he made his way through the rows of
tents out of the camp, and entered the ruins of Jericho. By the
moonlight he carefully made his way through the debris until
he reached the vicinity of the street where the shops had been
located.

There he began his search through the ruins until he
found what he was looking for, silver, gold, and precious
stones which adorned the Babylonian garments. Now quietly,
cautiously, he retraced his steps back to the camp with his
loot. You will recall that God had issued a ban against any
such action. The people had been warned in Joshua 6:18,
"But as for you, only keep yourselves from the things under the
ban, lest you covet them and take some of the things under the
ban, so you would make the camp of Israel accursed and bring
trouble on it." Therefore, this action by Achan was an act of
outright rebellion and disobedience.

Upon reaching his tent, he quickly dashed in, grabbed a
spade, and began to dig a hole in the ground at the rear of his
tent. He filled the hole with the valuables, covered it over, and

lay down on his cot, congratulating himself on such a daring expedition. No one had seen him. No one, that is, but the all-seeing eye of the Lord God of Israel!

This solitary act of rebellion against God brought a major setback for the entire nation of Israel. There is much to be learned in this chapter. All of us are familiar with defeat, and although it is not necessary, it is unfortunately rather common. God has carefully recorded this account in the Scriptures so our eyes may be opened to the sources, side effects, and solutions of setbacks. This is our SOS chapter because it deals with solving our setbacks. If defeat comes, these truths can lead us into victory when applied by faith. How do we solve our setbacks? What can we do when setbacks come? First of all, we must:

ACKNOWLEDGE THE SOURCE
OF OUR SETBACKS
(Josh. 7:1-3)

In many cases the primary source of our setbacks is *self-reliance*. Such is the case before us.

> "But the sons of Israel acted unfaithfully in regard to the things under the ban, for Achan . . . took some of the things under the ban, therefore the anger of the Lord burned against the sons of Israel. Now Joshua sent men from Jericho to Ai, which is near Bethaven, east of Bethel, and said to them, 'Go up and spy out the land.' So the men went up and spied out Ai" (Josh. 7:1-2).

Early in this volume, we noticed the frequency of the words, "And the Lord said to Joshua." However, as we come to chapter 7 of Joshua, we find these words are strangely missing. As we reach verse 2 it is quite clear that Joshua failed to wait on God. Between verses 1 and 2, we should have been reading of a great prayer meeting at Gilgal.

Do you know what happened to Joshua and those Israelites? They forgot that God defeated Jericho for them. They had lapsed into the thinking that they had won the battle themselves. They became self-reliant. And that is usually the first step toward defeat. We are prone to be exactly like that, aren't we? One of our greatest temptations after God gives us a smashing victory is neglect of prayer. If we aren't careful, self-reliance will set in instead of God-reliance. This is a sure source of setback.

Following the text further, we see that another root of our setbacks is *self-confidence*. The men went up and spied out Ai. "And they returned to Joshua and said to him, 'Do not let all the people go up; only about two or three thousand men need go up to Ai; do not make all the people toil up there, for they are few' " (Josh. 7:3). The children of Israel let *self*-confidence instead of *God*-confidence set in after that victory at Jericho.

Ai was a much smaller city, not nearly as well fortified. It would be easy to destroy, and they "reasoned" a few thousand men was all that would be needed. All of their thinking was based on the supposition that Israel had defeated Jericho. They were self-confident and forgot what God had done for them! An interesting insight is found in verse 2, "Now Joshua sent men." Do you see the difference? Before, God had been sending them. Now God wasn't sending them at all—Joshua was doing the sending. And they were going with confidence only in the flesh. They began to think they were really somebody.

There is no experience in the Christian walk as dangerous as that period immediately following a great victory. That is, *after revival comes*. If we are not careful it will open the door for self-confidence. The Israelites thought that yesterday's victory (at Jericho) would suffice for today's commitment (at Ai), and they were tragically mistaken. Some of us meet our setbacks in the same fashion. The victory comes, accompanied by glory and power, the mountaintop! But if we are not cautious, we are so inclined to self-confidence. Self-confidence is a certain source of setbacks.

There is yet another cause of our setbacks, *self-centered-*

ness. Achan is a number-one prime example of this source of setback. When later confronted by Joshua, Achan revealed the heart of his problem by saying:

> Truly, *I* have sinned against the Lord, the God of Israel, and this is what *I* did; when *I* saw among the spoil a beautiful mantle from Shinar and two hundred shekels of silver and a bar of gold fifty shekels in weight, then *I* coveted them and [*I*] took them; and behold, [*I*] concealed them in the earth inside my tent with the silver underneath it (Josh. 7:20-21).

Note the number of times the personal pronoun "I" is used. Here is self-centeredness at its worst. Here was a certain source of setbacks. Note the progression in Achan's setback. "I saw . . . I coveted . . .[I] took . . . [I] concealed!" If you recall, this is exactly what brought Adam and Eve's downfall. They saw, they coveted, they took, and then they hid from a holy God! It is the devil's tactic for bringing about your defeat. Self-centeredness is a sure source of setback.

Let's come close and personal again. Are you living under the load of some setback right now? Have you suffered some defeat? Be still a moment and acknowledge the source of your setback. You will never solve your setbacks without first acknowledging their source. And when you and I do, most likely it will be the result of self-reliance, self-confidence, or self-centeredness.

When setbacks come, we should not only acknowledge their source, but we should also;

ASCERTAIN THE SIDE EFFECTS
OF OUR SETBACKS
(Josh. 7:4-9)

What are the side effects of our setbacks? First of all, a setback *brings defeat*. "And the men of Ai struck down about thirty-six of their men and pursued them from the gate as far as Shebarim, and struck them down on the descent, so the hearts of the people melted and became as water" (Josh. 7:5). There was only one Achan in the camp, but all Israel was defeated because of his sin. About thirty-six Israelites were killed, and the rest ran like cowards. Defeat is sure to follow disobedience. It is a side effect of setbacks.

Who can tell how much the advancement of Christ's kingdom is hindered because there are Achans in the camp. To whatever extent you are disobedient and live according to the world's standards, to the same extent you hinder the work of the church and hold up the forward progress of God's army.

Now, notice that a chain reaction was set into motion. Our setbacks present defeat, which in turn *brings discouragement.*

> "Then Joshua tore his clothes and fell to the earth on his face before the ark of the Lord until the evening, both he and the elders of Israel; and they put dust on their heads. And Joshua said, 'Alas, O Lord God, why didst Thou ever bring this people over the Jordan, only to deliver us into the hand of the Amorites, to destroy us? If only we had been willing to dwell beyond the Jordan!' " (Josh. 7:6-7).

Can't you see Joshua? Discouragement had set in. "Oh no, we're going to be slaughtered. Good grief, we're never going to get out of this mess. Mercy, it would be better if we had never come into this land at all. We should have stayed on the other side of the Jordan."

When defeat comes, we are inclined to get down and to become discouraged. I've been there, haven't you? It's easy to fix our eyes on the problem when defeat comes and to lapse into discouragement. Discouragement is a devastating side effect to setbacks.

As we study the text we follow the progression and note that defeat brings discouragement, which in turn, *brings doubt.* " 'Oh Lord, what can I say since Israel has turned their back before their enemies? For the Canaanites and all the inhabitants of the land will hear of it, and they will surround us and cut off our name from the earth. And what wilt Thou do for Thy great name?' " (Josh. 7:8-9). Joshua was not only defeated, and discouraged, but he began to doubt God. "Oh me, everyone is going to hear about this. All the Canaanites will hear about this and they will wipe us out." Joshua doubted that victory would ever come again.

Doubt is deadly! If Satan can only cause us to doubt, over half of his battle is already won. If we are not cautious, doubt is a sure result. All we need do is wallow in our discouragement long enough, and we'll soon find ourselves settled into doubt. Incidentally, do you know how to deal with doubt? We deal with it like we would any other sin. Confess it and forsake it!

The final side effect is the most devastating of the whole chain reaction. Setbacks bring defeat, which brings discouragement, which brings doubt, which *brings dishonor*. "And what wilt Thou do for Thy great name?" (Josh. 7:9). The most tragic element about sinful setbacks is that they bring dishonor to the name of the Lord. When Achan sinned and caused Israel's defeat at Ai, the most damaging effect was the dishonor to the name of the Lord.

Why should we want to see people saved? Not primarily because they would be better husbands or wives or parents or associates or citizens. It is not primarily because they can escape hell and inherit heaven. The underlying motive for seeing people come to accept Christ as Savior and Lord should be that by their coming to him, they might no longer trample under foot the grace of Jesus poured out on Calvary, and dishonor his name in the process.

By coming to Christ, they would give him considerable honor and glory. This is the overreaching reason for our emphasis upon all of us being "Canaan Christians." You see, wilderness Christians who live in their own strength, holding to the world with one hand and God with the other, dishonor his holy name.

Are you hampered by a setback? Are you suffering from defeat? Be still a moment. Isn't the text right? Is your life

characterized by those side effects? defeat? discouragement?
doubt? dishonor?

What should we do about it? How do we deal with and
solve our setbacks? Where is the SOS? After all, it is one thing
to acknowledge their source and ascertain their side effects,
but we must know how to deal with them and put them
away. Let's hasten on to:

APPLY THE SOLUTION TO OUR SETBACKS
(Josh. 7:10-26)
The first step in solving our setbacks is *conviction*.

> "So the Lord said to Joshua, 'Rise up! Why is it that you
> have fallen on your face? Israel has sinned, and they have
> also transgressed My covenant which I commanded them.
> And they have even taken some of the things under the ban
> and have both stolen and deceived. Moreover, they have
> also put them among their own things. Therefore, the sons
> of Israel cannot stand before their enemies; they turn their
> backs before their enemies, for they have become accursed. I
> will not be with you any more unless you destroy the things
> under the ban from your midst' " (Josh. 7:10-12).

God said, "Joshua, get up! Why are you crying and feeling sorry for yourself? Now get up! This is not the time to
pray!" Why would God tell Joshua to quit praying? The
answer—prayer without repentance has no victory. God said,
"Israel has sinned." Now wait a moment. I thought Achan
sinned and now God is passing judgment on all Israel. I trust
the Holy Spirit will write this lesson across our hearts. If we
are a member of the body of Christ, we cannot sin without its
affecting the whole body.

For thirty-three years, the world looked upon the physical
body of Jesus Christ. They watched him. They listened to
him. They saw that he practiced everything he preached. In
our world today, born-again believers make up the body of
Christ. We each have a specific part in this great body. We

each have a function. But I fear we are giving the world an extremely anemic picture of the lover of our souls. I am thankful that I have a healthy body, physically.

There are at least three functions I expect from my body. I expect every member to be present. I cannot function as I ought without every member of my body present and accounted for. I also expect every member to be healthy. When infection sets into a sore on my foot, my whole body begins to ache. It affects me all over. If I am to function to my ultimate capabilities, I need every member, not only present but every member healthy. I also expect every member to be obedient. When my brain sends a message to my hand to pick up my pen and begin to write, I expect my hand to be obedient to the command of my head. I simply cannot function to my best capability unless every member is obedient. Now, if I expect that of my physical body, why should Jesus Christ have to expect anything less of his body—you and me?

I trust the Holy Spirit will brand this upon your heart. We cannot sin without affecting the whole body. The testimony of the church throughout the community and throughout the world depends on the victorious Christian life of every one of us! Every one of us is important.

God continued, "I will not be with you any more unless you destroy the things" (v. 12). What conviction this wrought! The thought of the removal of the blessing of God is sobering indeed. All of this thrust Joshua to his senses and convicted him of sin in the camp.

But it is not enough merely to be convicted of our sin. The second step in applying the solution to our setbacks is *consecration*, sanctification! "Rise up! Consecrate the people and say, 'Consecrate yourselves for tomorrow, for thus the Lord, the God of Israel has said, "There are things under the ban in your midst, O Israel. You cannot stand before your enemies until you have removed the things under the ban from your midst" (Josh. 7:13).

God commanded, "Clean up!" What does it mean to be

"sanctified"? It is the experience in which the cleansing process is set in motion to purge us of sin and conform us to the image of Jesus. And how are we to be sanctified? Note the text, "Consecrate yourselves!" God will not overrule our will. He will convict us; he will draw us by his precious Spirit, but he will not confess our sins for us.

Note expecially God's words in verse 13, "You cannot stand before your enemies until you have removed the things under the ban from your midst." Here is a call to repentance, to change our minds about the solution to our setbacks. There can be no victory, no solving our setbacks, no consecration, unless there is repentance!

As we follow the text, we see that there is another step in solving our setbacks, *compliance!*

> "In the morning then you shall come near by your tribes. And it shall be that the tribe which the Lord takes by lot shall come near by families, and the family which the Lord takes shall come near by households, and the household which the Lord takes shall come near man by man. And it shall be that the one who is taken with the things under the ban shall be burned with fire, he and all that belongs to him, because he has transgressed the covenant of the Lord, and because he has committed a disgraceful thing in Israel.' So Joshua arose early in the morning and brought Israel near by tribes, and the tribe of Judah was taken" (Josh. 7:14-16).

God had given an order and Joshua was obedient! He "arose early in the morning" and complied with God's command. If there is one thing that keeps recurring throughout the pages of the Book of Joshua, it is the importance of being obedient. This is where many of us fall and fail. Oh, how we need this element of compliance in our lives!

And then we note there is a final step, *confession!*

> "Then Joshua said to Achan, 'My son, I implore you, give glory to the Lord, the God of Israel, and give praise to Him; and tell me now what you have done. Do not hide it

from me.' So Achan answered Joshua and said, 'Truly, I have sinned against the Lord, the God of Israel, and this is what I did; when I saw among the spoil a beautiful mantle from Shinar and two hundred shekels of silver and a bar of gold fifty shekels in weight, I coveted them and took them; and behold, they are concealed in the earth inside my tent with the silver underneath it' " (Josh. 7:19-21).

As I spent hours in this text, I literally came to tears every time I approached these verses. I feel with Achan. When he watched the army of God retreat, he knew he was to blame. When he saw those thirty-six friends killed in battle, his poor conscience was racked with the thought that he was responsible.

Do you see him standing before Joshua? Listen to his confession, "Joshua, I saw . . . I coveted . . . I took . . . I hid . . . Oh Joshua, I acknowledge my sin."

Confession is essential to solving our setbacks. You may be living in the middle of setbacks and defeat right now because you have not admitted your sin and confessed it to God. The Bible says, "Who confesses and forsakes [his sin] will find compassion" (Prov. 28:13).

Are you suffering from a defeat? If so, apply the solution to your setback—conviction, consecration, compliance, and confession.

I must add that we find a rather shocking result in this whole episode.

"Then Joshua and all Israel with him, took Achan the son of Zerah, the silver, the mantle, the bar of gold, his sons, his daughters, his oxen, his donkeys, his sheep, his tent and all that belonged to him; and they brought them up to the valley of Achor. And Joshua said, 'Why have you troubled us? The Lord will trouble you this day.' And all Israel stoned them with stones; and they burned them with fire after they had stoned them with stones. And they raised over him a great heap of stones that stands to this day, and the Lord turned from the fierceness of his anger. Therefore the name of that place has been called the valley of Achor to this day" (Josh. 7:24-26).

Now, that is extremely firm discipline, to say the least! But we have not gotten the point at all unless we understand that on Jesus Christ God poured all the sin of the world and he died bearing it in his own body on the tree. God is as serious about sin today as he was then.

Sin is serious! Some of us are foolish to think we are getting away with our sins just because judgment doesn't fall the moment we sin. God is hard on sin! He hates sin! Sin put his only Son on the cross. We should not be so foolish as to think we can continually sow seeds of sin and escape judgment by merely praying for a crop failure!

We are alive—and perhaps well today because of the mercy of God. The only reason you and I don't suffer the same punishment of Achan is that we live in a day of grace. Not a one of us deserves to be here. If we got what we deserved, in ten seconds every one of us would be burning in a literal hell. But God is rich in mercy and grace.

As we leave the children of Israel, we see them on their way to victory once more. Chapter 8 begins with God promising, "I will be with you. Go on over to Ai; I have given it to you. Victory is yours!"

Dear reader, you may have had a setback, but you can go away from this volume with your sins forgiven. God is ready to meet you on his terms. Here is the way: *Acknowledge the source of your setbacks*; self-reliance, self-confidence, self-centeredness! *Ascertain the side effects of your setbacks*; defeat, discouragement, doubt, dishonor! *Apply the solution to your setbacks*; conviction, consecration, compliance, and confession!

Go ahead, apply that solution to your setbacks today and let God assure you, "I will be with you. Go on over to Ai; I have given it to you." Victory is yours, and can stay yours *after revival comes.*

GETTING USED TO THE
FAMILY OF GOD

Jim didn't have much to live for the first time we saw him. Our evangelism team knocked on his door one night. Shirtless and with a beer in his hand, he invited us into his one-room rental apartment. Twin beds filled the room; one for Jim and the other for his two small boys, already fast asleep in each other's arms. Jim was literally fighting for survival, working ten hours a day as a carpenter, picking up the boys from the day-care center, and going home to be dad and mom as best he could. His situation seemed hopeless. Like many singles in our city, he was overcome with loneliness in the midst of over one million people.

We invaded Jim's privacy that night, but he didn't seem to mind. Desperation has a way of breaking a person. It wasn't long until Jim's lonely, heartbroken life was filled with the ever-abiding love of Jesus himself.

A sweet young couple, the Micklers, "adopted" Jim and the boys. They were smart enough to know that you can't just toss the baby bottle into the crib and expect the newborn babe to feed himself. Time and again they put the "bottle" in Jim's mouth and he began to grow in Jesus. The Micklers were always there, when Jim was lonely, when he almost cut off his hand on the job, when one of the boys had surgery, when Jim's family had no place to go on the holidays.

Has Jesus made a difference in Jim? Today, he owns his own home. He is on our church staff full time. He has led both of his boys to Jesus. He leads an evangelism team on Thursday evenings. And he gives in excess of a double tithe to advance the kingdom through our First Baptist Church.

Incidentally, Jim still needs the Micklers and they still need him. The truth is, we all need each other. "If any man is in Christ, he is a new creature; the old things passed away; behold, new things have come" (2 Cor. 5:17). *After Revival Comes.*

Chapter 6
THE WONDERFUL WALK
OF VICTORY

CHAPTER 6
The Wonderful Walk of Victory
(Galatians 5:19-26)

I. Problems That Hinder (19-21)

    A. Desires That Are Misdirected
"Now the deeds of the flesh are evident, which are: immorality, impurity, sensuality" (v. 19).

    B. Devotions That Are Misguided
"idolatry, sorcery . . ." (v. 20a).

    C. Dispositions That Are Mismanaged
"enmities, strife, jealousy, outbursts of anger, disputes, dissensions, factions,
envyings" (vv. 20b-21a).

II. Proofs That Highlight (22-23)

    A. A Countenance That Is Obvious
"love, joy, peace,

    B. A Conduct That Is Orderly
patience, kindness, goodness,

    C. A Character That Is Obedient
faithfulness,
gentleness, self-control" (vv. 22-23).

III. Procedures That Help (24-26)

    A. An Appropriation to Experience
"Now those who belong to Christ Jesus have crucified the flesh with its passions and desires" (v. 24).

112

B. An Action to Exhibit
"If we live by the Spirit, let us also walk by the Spirit" (v. 25).

C. An Attitude to Escape
"Let us not become boastful, challenging one another, envying one another" (v. 26).

The Wonderful Walk of Victory

Now the deeds of the flesh are evident, which are immorality, impurity, sensuality, idolatry, sorcery, enmities, strife, jealousy, outbursts of anger, disputes, dissensions, factions,

envyings, drunkenness, carousings, and things like these, of which I forewarn you just as I have forewarned you that those who practice such things shall not inherit the kingdom of God.

But the fruit of the Spirit is love, joy, peace, patience, kindness, goodness, faithfulness,

gentleness, self-control; against such things there is no law.

Now those who belong to Christ Jesus have crucified the flesh with its passions and desires.

If we live by the Spirit, let us also walk by the Spirit.

Let us not become boastful, challenging one another, envying one another. (Gal. 5:19-26).

Stuart Briscoe says that the life of the average Christian could be likened to an old iron bed, firm on both ends, but sagging in the middle. I think he is right! My great-aunt in Tennessee had an old iron bed during my boyhood days. It was a beauty to behold, sturdy and strong, but oh, that sagging middle! Have you ever slept in a sagging bed? Somehow I

THE WONDERFUL WALK OF VICTORY

always managed to end up in a ball in the middle! That old bed was firm on both ends, but what a middle!

Think about it. We are like that, aren't we? Most of us are firm on the front end. That is, we realize we've been saved. We look back to that day and with abounding confidence can testify "I know whom I have believed" (2 Tim. 1:12). And most of us are firm on the other end. That is, we know we are going to heaven when we die. But oh, that sagging middle! We may know we are going to heaven, but too few of us are having a heavenly time getting there.

The Bible refers to this period between conversion and heaven as the "walk" of the Christian. And it is not so much how far we walk, but *how* we walk that really matters. Many Christians are stumbling over all sorts of obstacles as they walk. Others are walking through dark valleys with little light. Still others seem to run up against all sorts of detours and dead ends!

God never intended the Christian walk to be one of discouragement, darkness, or defeat, but instead, a wonderful walk of victory, firm in the middle! This chapter is designed to lead us to that walk so we might enjoy it to the fullest. When appropriated, this exciting adventure will escort us out of the darkness and into the light. It will pull us away from our problems and into some tremendous possibilities. And it will turn our defeats into deliverance.

As we begin our walk it is important to note initially some

PROBLEMS THAT HINDER
(Gal. 5:19-21)

Earlier, I alluded to the fact that there are many Christians who are defeated in their walk. Have you ever really wondered why? It is because Satan has placed problems in our paths. Among these are *desires that are misdirected*. These misdirected desires consist of immorality, impurity, and sensuality (Gal. 5:19). Certainly, these are the works of the flesh and not of God. Immorality consists of adultery, fornication, homosexuality, and the like. Impurities deal more in the realm of our thought life, the lusts of the flesh conjured up in the mind. Sensuality is the idea of one who is so far gone in lust or forbidden desire that he no longer cares what people say or think about him.

There are many who aren't walking in victory because of these misdirected desires. We live in a day when an increasing number of people are wallowing in immorality and filth, a day when virginity and purity seem to be out of date. It is no longer uncommon in the major cities of our nation for over one-half of the babies to be born out of wedlock.

Why do you think God said, "You shall not commit adultery"? (Ex. 20:14). Was it to keep us from having any fun or to rob us of some satisfaction? Not at all! God gave us this Commandment because he loves us. He knew if we lived in shameful immorality, adultery, fornication, or the like, we would be miserable. Therefore, for our own good, He commanded it so we might have a happy and fruitful life.

Other hindrances to the wonderful walk of victory are *devotions that are misguided.* The Bible lists some of the misguided devotions as idolatry and sorcery (Gal. 5:20). Sorcery comes from the same word from which we derive the word *pharmacy,* and it had to do with the use of drugs even then in Paul's day. Idolatry is the worship of gods which the hands of men have made. Idolatry is one of the massive problems in America today. We may not be bowing down to an idol like some Oriental religionists do. We may not be wringing the neck of a scrawny chicken while the blood spills out over some grotesque mud idol like some of the natives in the bush country. But many of us are bowing down every week to the gods of this world, our hobbies, our jobs, and all sorts of petty idols. Our idol, or our god, is that which demands the center of our attention and devotion. It could even be a person in our life.

Why do you think God said, "You shall have no other gods before me"? (Ex. 20:3). Was it because he was so egotistical he demanded that everyone bow down to him? Was it because he wanted us to be miserable? No, a thousand times no! He knew that the only way we would ever have total happiness would be to crown him Lord. He gave us this Commandment because he loves us and wants the best for us.

The text lists some other hindrances to the wonderful walk of victory as *dispositions that are mismanaged.* These are enmities, strife, jealousy, outbursts of anger, disputes, dissensions, factions, envyings, drunkenness, carousings" (Gal. 5:20-21).

Enmities has to do with someone who is characteristically hostile toward other persons. It is the exact opposite of the Christian virtue of love. Strife means quarrelings and contentions. Jealousy is a desire to have what someone else has. Outbursts of anger means the disposition of a temper. Show me someone who is always blowing up on the outside, and I will in every case show you someone who does not have it all together on the inside. Disputes means self-seeking. A person who is always self-seeking is never a blessing to anyone. Dissensions—standing apart, flying apart instead of coming together. Factions—people with different views who end up disliking each other. Envyings is the spirit which grudges the fact that someone else has something. An envying person does not so much want the thing for himself, but simply does not want the other person to have it. Drunkenness and carousing is unrestrained, degenerate revelry.

How prone we are to be characterized by these dispositions that are mismanaged. It is no wonder that more of us are not walking the wonderful walk of victory.

There are multitudes of Christians living in defeat and frustration (sagging in the middle), and the reason set forth in our text is glaringly obvious. There are problems which hinder our walk, and until they are dealt with our walk will be a frustrating crawl of defeat instead of a wonderful walk of victory. Watch out for these obstacles along the road—desires that are misdirected, devotions that are misguided, and dispositions that are mismanaged. After wisely cautioning us concerning these problems, the text then sets forth some:

PROOFS THAT HIGHLIGHT
(Gal. 5:22-23)

If we are to walk in victory, our lives will be characterized by the fruit of the Spirit which is listed in Galatians 5:22-23. Paul termed the problems which hinder our walk as "deeds [plural] of the flesh" (Gal. 5:19). And then as he turned our attention to some proofs that highlight the walk, he referred to them as the "fruit [singular] of the Spirit" (Gal. 5:22).

At first glance one would think it is an obvious grammatical error, "The fruit of the Spirit *is* love, joy, peace, patience, kindness, goodness, faithfulness, gentleness, self-control" (vv. 22-23). But Paul was absolutely correct! You see, the works of the flesh are separate acts committed by people. They are works, while the ninefold fruit of the Spirit is the outcropping of one life within us. The fruit of the Spirit is beyond the power of man to produce, for it is inwrought and outworked by the Holy Spirit himself. Can you grasp it? Being comes before doing. The fruit is *what we are* rather than what we do!

The fruit of the Spirit, which are the proofs that highlight the wonderful walk of victory, is divisible into three sections. The first triad—love, joy, and peace—deals with our relationship to God, our upward expression. The second triad—patience, kindness, goodness—deals with our relationship to others, our outward expression. And the final trio—faithfulness, gentleness, self-control—deals with our relationship to ourselves, our inward expression. Oh how wonderfully comprehensive is the fruit of the Spirit wrought in us by the Holy Spirit!

As we observe these proofs, we see that the first proof of one's really walking in victory is a *countenance that is obvious.* One's face will have love, joy, and peace written all over it! Are you walking the walk of victory? If so, you will have a countenance that is obvious.

The initial proof of it will be love. Before we can truly grasp the importance of this first proof, we must understand the word used in the text. In the Greek there are several words which are translated into the English word *love*. One of these is *eros*, which means sexual love between a man and a woman. It is a passionate love. Another word for love is *philos* which is the love for our nearest and dearest. It is a feeling of the heart.

There is also the word *agape*. This is God's love. This love means that, no matter what someone may do to us by insult, injury, or humiliation, we will never seek anything else but their highest good. And this is the word used in Galatians 5:22! One of the proofs is that we will love others in spite of what they may have done to us.

It is no coincidence that love is given first place in the list of the fruit, since all of the other manifestations of the fruit are various forms of love. Love is the foundation of all the others.

Another characteristic of the countenance that is obvious is joy. The Spirit produces joy in the lives of those who trust him. The word does not imply the type of joy that comes from defeating an opponent or in having no trouble. It is the joy that only God can give, even in the midst of sorrow. Christ was a "man of sorrows," but he was anointed with the "oil of gladness."

There is another proof that will highlight and set apart those who in reality walk with God—and that is peace. This is the inner harmony and tranquillity that the Spirit-filled believer enjoys. It is the peace Jesus talked about in the upper room when he said, "My peace I give to you; not as the world gives do I give to you. Let not your heart be troubled nor let it be fearful" (John 14:27).

What about your countenance? Do you radiate love, joy, and peace? Too many of us walk the Christian life, looking as if we have acid indigestion or a migraine headache most of the time. Those who really walk with God will be known by their countenance—love, joy, and peace.

Not only is there a countenance that is obvious for those who walk in the Spirit, but another proof is *a conduct that is orderly*. It is expressed in the word *patience, kindness*, and

goodness. Patience denotes longsuffering toward people, perhaps even those who persecute you. It implies a refusal to
retaliate. I suppose love's greatest victory is attained not in
what love does, but in what love refrains from doing. Patience
is the first expression of an orderly conduct.

Kindness is a disposition which expresses God's attitude
toward people. Kindness or gentleness is not a weak quality
but it is power on reserve. A proof of those who walk the wonderful walk of victory is certainly a gentle spirit.

Goodness was so characteristic of Jesus who "went about
doing good." Like Jesus, the Spirit-filled believer will allow the
Holy Spirit to produce the fruit of goodness through his life.

Finally, the walk of victory will be evidenced by a *character that is obedient.* It is expressed in the words *faithfulness,
gentleness,* and *self-control. Faithfulness* is not the type of
faith expressed in belief in God in view here. It is rather the
faithful discharge of entrusted duties. The person who walks
the wonderful walk of victory will have an obedient character
expressed primarily in dependability and faithful men to his
tasks.

Gentleness implies anger on a leash. The same word is
used for an animal which has been domesticated and is at his
master's command. It is not a milquetoast, passive type of
gentleness. It is quiet, reserved firmness. Self-control literally
means holding in with a firm hand. It has been designed as
the mastering of one's passions. But we must not forget that
this fruit of the Spirit, self-control in particular, is not the
working of the flesh's energy but the inworking of the Holy
Spirit within us.

May I become personal for a moment? Do people look at
you and see these proofs—love, joy, peace, patience, kindness,
goodness, faithfulness, gentleness, self-control? If not, why
not? The Holy Spirit yearns to produce them in you. Oh, perhaps you are saying, "I want to walk in victory. I want people
to see these proofs in me. I long for a countenance that is obvious, a conduct that is orderly, and a character that is obedient. But how can I be so transformed as to have the fruit of

the Spirit burst forth through my life!"

As always the Scripture does not leave without the "how to" of walking the wonderful walk of victory. Not only does it warn us of problems that hinder our walk, not only does it reveal the proofs that highlight our walk, but finally it leaves us with some:

PROCEDURES THAT HELP
(Gal. 5:24-26)

First of all, there is an *appropriation to experience*. It is found in verse 24. "Now those who belong to Christ Jesus have crucified the flesh with its passions and desires." No person has ever walked the wonderful walk of victory without putting self aside and reckoning it as dead. We must realize that those of us who have been saved have entered into Christ's death. Our part now is to *reckon* ourselves as dead indeed unto sin but alive unto God through Christ Jesus. We need to appropriate what is already ours. There is an appropriation to experience.

What about you? Have you experienced this death to self? Or are you living strictly in the flesh? If so, I know something about you. There are some problems that are hindering your walk. When we live in the flesh, we are usually characterized by misdirected desires, misguided devotions, or mismanaged dispositions. God calls us today to reckon with Paul, "I have been crucified with Christ; and it is no longer I who live, but Christ lives in me" (Gal. 2:20).

There not only is an appropriation to experience but there is also an *action to exhibit!* "If we live by the Spirit, let us also walk by the Spirit" (Gal. 5:25). We are not merely to talk a good game. We are to walk a good game! This implies action. If we are walking in the Spirit we will not be wearing out the seats of our pants, but the soles of our shoes. The Christ alive in us will be in the process being released through us.

My wife and I have the thrill of traveling and preaching in Israel each year. That tiny bit of earth where "God was in

Christ reconciling the world unto himself" is certainly "the Holy Land." There are two main bodies of water in that land, one in the north known as the Sea of Galilee and the other in the south, the Dead Sea.

The Sea of Galilee is one of the most beautiful bodies of water in the world. It is teeming with life, vibrant, and indescribably refreshing. Quite to the contrary, The Dead Sea lives up to its name. It is the lowest spot on the earth. It contains practically no aquatic life, and its smell is nauseating. Why the stark difference in these two water bodies? The reason is obvious.

The Jordan River has its source at the foot of Mount Hermon in the far north. From there it flows south and empties into the Sea of Galilee. It makes its exit on the southern shore, and the river continues south until it empties into the Dead Sea which has no outlet. And that is precisely the problem. The Sea of Galilee "takes in" but it also "gives out," and therefore is vibrant and alive. The Dead Sea "takes in" but has no outlet, which makes it stagnant and dead. Need I say more? "If we live by the Spirit, let us also walk by the Spirit" (Gal. 5:25). If we "take in" of the Spirit, let us "give out" of the Spirit.

I am concerned over those folks who spend all their time "taking in." They have cassette tapes, books, and pamphlets, but they seem to be nothing more than spiritual sponges. They never let the Spirit release himself through their lives in action to a lost and dying world. Friends, Jesus said, "If we live by the Spirit, let us also walk by the Spirit!"

There is an action to exhibit. I challenge you today to put action to your faith. It is the only means of overcoming these problems that hinder our walk. In verse 16 we read, "But I say, walk by the Spirit and you will not carry out the desire of the flesh." When we are in the service of Jesus, we will not have time for the desires of the flesh. Are you anxious to overcome these problems that hinder? Then walk in the Spirit!

There is a final procedure which helps our walk, and that is the realization that there is *an attitude to escape.* "Let us not become boastful, challenging one another, envying one another" (Gal. 5:26). Think about it a moment! Now what do we really have to boast about anyway? Our bank accounts? Big deal! Fifty years from now every penny of it will be deposited in someone else's name. Our position? So what? Someone else has a better one. Our new home? In a few years it will rot. We really have nothing to boast about. We are nothing without God. The very best we are is as filthy rags alongside the righteousness of the holy God. Self and ego have no place in the wonderful walk of victory. They tend to exalt self instead of Jesus. This is an attitude to escape.

Another attitude to escape is that of challenging and envying one another. There is no room in the wonderful walk of victory for this attitude. This attitude is really saying, "I don't necessarily want what someone has—I just don't want them to have it." That reasoning will defeat you. And once again, we see that the root of the problem is the old nature—the flesh, the ego. Oh, what an attitude to escape!

In conclusion, let's retrace our walk. Are you firm at the head end? Are you sure of your salvation? If not, then repent of your sins now. Ask God's forgiveness and invite Jesus Christ into your heart as Savior and Lord. And what about the other end? Do you know for sure that you are going to heaven? If so, you do not have to be like that old iron bed, sagging in the middle. You can walk the wonderful walk of victory every moment of every day.

But remember as you go, there are some problems that will hinder—desires that are misdirected, devotions that are misguided, dispositions that are mismanaged. And if you are really walking in the Spirit, people will know it, not by your telling them but by the proofs that will highlight your walk. You will have a countenance that is obvious, a conduct that is orderly, and a character that is obedient.

And how is all of this attainable? What are the procedures that help the wonderful walk of victory? There is an appropriation to experience (death to self), there is an action to exhibit (if you live in the Spirit, then walk in the Spirit), and there is an attitude to avoid (stay positive and do not become boastful and envious—).

The road is before you. Why not start the wonderful walk of victory right now? Go ahead, Jesus has paved the way. In fact, he is The Way! Holiness is not the way to Jesus. Jesus is the way to holiness. You can make it, right now, by faith!

THE LAND OF BEGINNING AGAIN!

Barry was a sight to behold when he sauntered up to our church on a Sunday morning. His eyes were red from lack of sleep, his body bent from the weight of the large backpack he was carrying, and he was hungry. One of our ushers spotted him out front and gave him a warm welcome, a doughnut, and a hot cup of coffee. Barry couldn't believe that a well-dressed, Gentile Baptist could care anything about a down-and-out Jewish boy on the run!

Drawn by this unconditional love and acceptance, Barry decided to stay for church to see why this man would care so much. Like Todd, mentioned earlier, the love of Jesus began constraining Barry. After church some of our singles got Barry a place to stay. He began coming to the services and reading a Bible. He soon learned that we Baptists were not asking him to convert to our religion. The truth is, we had converted to his! The Lord Jesus is indeed the promised Messiah. Barry received him as his own personal Savior and at this writing, two years later, he is still here and growing taller in the faith with each passing day.

Barry is part of the family of God today because an usher at a high-steepled, downtown church cared enough to walk across the street to say welcome. Folks love the unlovely and take serious the commandment of Jesus to carry the gospel to the poor, "After Revival Comes."

Chapter 7
GETTING IN . . . AND
GOING ON!

CHAPTER 7
Getting In . . . and Going On!
(1 Kings 17:1-7)

At the brook Cherith, we see:

I. God's Recognized Plan (1-3)

"Now Elijah . . .
The word of the Lord came to him saying,
'Go away from here and " 'hide yourself by the brook Cherith' "
(vv. 1-3).

II. God's Restricted Promise (4)

"And it shall be that you shall drink of the brook, and I have
commanded the ravens to provide for you there" (v. 4).

III. God's Required Prerequisite (5)

"So he went and did according to the word of the Lord, for he
went and lived by the brook Cherith, which is east of the Jordan"
(v. 5).

IV. God's Released Provision (6)

"And the ravens brought him bread and meat in the morning
and bread and meat in the evening, and he would drink from the
brook" (v. 6).

V. God's Revealed Purpose (7)

"And it happened after a while, that the brook dried up, because
there was no rain in the land" (v. 7).

Getting In . . . and Going On

> Now Elijah the Tishbite, who was of the settlers of
> Gilead, said to Ahab, "As the Lord, the God of Israel lives,
> before whom I stand, surely there shall be neither dew nor
> rain these years, except by my word."
> And the word of the Lord came to him, saying,
> "Go away from here and turn eastward, and hide your-
> self by the brook Cherith, which is east of the Jordan.
> "And it shall be that you shall drink of the brook, and I
> have commanded the ravens to provide for you there."
> So he went and did according to the word of the Lord,
> for he went and lived by the brook Cherith, which is east of
> the Jordan.
> And the ravens brought him bread and meat in the
> morning and bread and meat in the evening, and he would
> drink from the brook.
> And it happened after a while, that the brook dried up,
> because there was no rain in the land (1 Kings 17:1-7).

Elijah is one of my favorite characters in the Bible. The
text of this chapter is the first mention of him in the Scriptures.
It is interesting that he is referred to initially as "Elijah the
Tishbite." This little-known, roughclad Tishbite from the
mountain region of Gilead was known by his previous envi-
ronment. But an amazing thing begins to unfold as we follow

the succeeding chapters of Scripture. After he has been on the scene for a while and the people begin to see God not only in him but on him, he is then referred to as "Elijah, the man of God" (1 Kings 17:18). He was no longer being identified from the region of his birth, but by his relationship with God. But then an unusual happening began to unfold near the end of his life. As people saw him walking down the street, the Scriptures tell us that they no longer referred to him as "Elijah, the Tishbite." Nor did they even refer to him any longer as "Elijah, the man of God." Near the end of his life, after all of the miraculous things wrought by God through him, as people saw him walking down the street, they simply exclaimed, "There goes the man of God!" He lost his previous identity.

Now the New Testament tells us that "Elijah was a man with a nature like ours" (Jas. 5:17). Plainly stated, you and I are made out of the same stuff as Elijah. He was weak where we are weak. He failed where we so often fail. But this man "with a nature like ours" entered into and applied tremendous truths in living which enabled him to enter, and go on to, a life of faith and victory which caught the attention of a nation. *After revival comes* it is imperative that we get in and go on.

What shaped and molded this man of God? What enabled him to live in such victory that he could call down fire from heaven on Mount Carmel? Where did he receive his strength to raise the widow's son at Zeraphath? Where did he get his boldness? What was his secret?

I believe we shall discover that this trip to the little brook Cherith was his most memorable journey. As our previous schooling prepared us for our life's vocation, the lessons of Cherith prepared Elijah for what lay ahead. There at the brook Cherith he learned the basics. There at the brook he built a foundation on which was to be erected a monumental work for God that turn a nation back to God.

We cannot bypass Cherith on our way toward the mountaintop experiences of Carmel. There must be a Cherith before there can be a Carmel. If we are to be men and women of

God, we must know something of this Cherith, an education in order to get in and go on, *after revival comes.* Let's journey together to Cherith, with the expectation that we will move from there and from this volume to some Mount Carmel experience for God.

First, at the brook Cherith we see:

GOD'S RECOGNIZED PLAN
(1 Kings 17:1-3)

One of the irresistible truths in the life of Elijah is how God "leads his dear children along." Elijah was standing before the wicked King Ahab. He was pronouncing God's judgment of a three-and-one-half-year drought upon the land. This announcement found little favor with the king. What would Elijah do now? Where would he seek refuge? Just at his moment of need, "The word of the Lord came to him, saying, 'Go away from here and turn eastward and hide yourself by the brook Cherith, which is east of the Jordan' " (1 Kings 17:2-3). As Elijah stayed sensitive to the voice of God, he was led by God.

The brook Cherith was one of several little brooks which flowed into the Jordan. It was and is located in that rugged, mountainous wilderness between Jerusalem and Jericho. Nestled in the bottom of huge rock cliffs, it was as secluded a spot as might be found. It was virtually shut off from the world. It was to such a place that God instructed Elijah to retreat.

"Go away from here and turn eastward, and hide yourself by the brook Cherith, which is east of Jordan" (1 Kings 17:3). The key word in God's recognized plan at Cherith is *hide.* He told Elijah to go and "hide" himself at the brook Cherith. The word here is not to be confused with the connotation of hiding from the enemy. For example, it is not he same word as used in Joshua 2 when "Rahab hid the spies." Rather, the word here has to do with taking time to reflect and retreat. It could well be rendered, "Turn thee eastward and absent thyself." So Elijah was not instructed to hide in order to protect himself from Ahab. God instructed him to come apart in order to reveal himself to Elijah, do business with him, and prepare him for what was ahead.

This plan is recognized throughout the Scriptures in the making of men and women of God. God always commands this of those who will be especially used by him. It is not new in the making of a man of God. Joseph had his "brook Cherith" before he became the preserver of his people and prime minister of Egypt. His brook Cherith was an Egyptian dungeon, but it prepared him to become the man of God.

Moses had his "brook Cherith," forty years of isolation in the desert. But it prepared him to be the great emancipator of his people.

Joshua had his "brook Cherith," forty years in the wilderness with Canaan in his heart. But it prepared him to be the man of God who could lead the children of Israel into the Promised Land.

The first-century apostles had their Cheriths before they became the pillars of the faith. On at least one occasion they returned to Jesus and thought they were somebody. They were full of pride and success. "And [Jesus] said to them, 'Come away by yourselves to a lonely place and rest a while" (Mark 6:31). These experiences added considerably in the making of them into the instruments of God.

The upper room served as the brook Cherith for a hundred and twenty people after the resurrection. Their Cherith was "to [tarry] in the city [of Jerusalem]" (Luke 24:49), to hide and wait for ten days until they were filled with power from on high. Evangelist Ron Dunn says it is at this very point where we see the difference in the first-century and the twentieth-century church. The first-century Christians prayed for *ten days*, Peter stood up and preached for *ten minutes*, and three thousand people were saved. Today we seem to have reversed the order. We pray for *ten minutes*, preach for *ten days*, see a few people saved, and run around exclaiming that we've had a Pentecost! We will never be men and women of God until we learn this principle of God's recognized plan.

And even our Lord Jesus had his brook Cherith, thirty years of silence and seclusion in the carpenter's shop, and then one day he burst from obscurity and changed the world. He spent thirty years in subjection to his parents, thirty years being faithful to his synagogue every week, thirty years of preparing faithfully for a ministry that was to last only three years. Jesus never forgot the Cherith experience. And before the cross, he found his Cherith amid the olive trees of Gethsemane, absenting himself in order to meet God!

Have you had a Cherith? Have you taken the time to "go eastward and hide" at your brook Cherith? It is an important step in God's recognized plan in the making of a man of God. Every one of God's children, if they are to live in victory, must find their strength in some hidden Cherith. Too many today want to make a success of themselves at Mount Carmel and call down fire from heaven. But too few are willing to pay the price at brook Cherith alone with God. Cherith always leads to Carmel. It is impossible to "give out" at a Carmel until we have "taken in" at a Cherith.

At the brook Cherith we see not only God's recognized plan for us but also:

GOD'S RESTRICTED PROMISE
(1 Kings 17:4)

Elijah received a promise from God, but like many of God's promises, it was restricted and conditional. Let's look closely at the promise. God instructed Elijah to go to the brook Cherith, and "it shall be that you shall drink of the brook and I have commanded the ravens to provide for you there." There is a strong emphasis on the word *there*.

It was "there," at the brook Cherith, that the ravens were instructed to feed Elijah. Suppose he had reasoned in his mind a better place to hide back in the mountain region of Gilead. After all, he grew up in that rugged terrain. Undoubtedly, he knew better places to hide than at Cherith. Suppose he had retreated back to the Gilead region. He would have starved to death and missed God, for the ravens had not been commanded to go there. Elijah could have "blown it" altogether if he had not been where God told him to be. God said, "I have commanded the ravens to provide for you *there* [at the brook Cherith]." It is an important thing, being where God tells us to be and doing what God tells us to do.

Before any of us can become men or women of God, we must be confronted with this question, "Am I where God wants me to be? Am I doing what God wants me to do?"

God has never promised to bless us if we are out of his will. "And it shall be that you shall drink of the brook, and I have commanded the ravens to provide for you there" (1 Kings 17:4). Many today are looking for victory. Many genuinely long to be men and women of God. But there is so little fruit, so little joy, so little blessing upon many lives. Could it be that God has promised to meet us "there" at the brook and we are somewhere else? Could it be that God has promised to meet us "there" in repentance, and we are somewhere else? Could it be that God has promised to meet us "there" in restitution, and we are somewhere else? Could it be that God has promised to meet us "there" in reconciliation, and we are somewhere else? Where is it that God has promised to meet you? God has promised to meet us "there" only—in the middle of his will. This is God's restricted promise.

At the brook Cherith we also see:

GOD'S REQUIRED PREREQUISITE
(1 Kings 17:5)

Along the route to becoming children of God there is an unavoidable prerequisite—obedience! Notice Elijah's response to the command of God to go to the brook Cherith. "*So he went and did* according to the word of the Lord, for he went and lived by the brook Cherith, which is east of Jordan" (1 Kings 17:5). Here is obedience to the word of God!

There was no defiance. He did not argue. He did not question. "So he went!" There was no delay! He did not prolong his journey. He did not postpone it. "So he went!" Also, there was no doubt. He showed no signs of disbelief. "So he went!" It is at this very point that so many of us often fall short. God speaks to our hearts, telling us to meet him at some secret place, and unlike Elijah we so often protest, "Lord, you can't mean there!"

It is important to note how Elijah went—"according to the word of the Lord." This, of course, is a direct reference back to verse 2, "And the word of the Lord came to him saying." He believed God and was obedient to God's word. This is God's required prerequisite in becoming a man of God, obedience! Some wonder why they have no faith. It is because they are not obedient to the revealed, personalized word of God to their hearts. "Faith comes from hearing, and hearing by the word of Christ" (Rom. 10:17).

Elijah could have reasoned away this word from God. But he didn't! It was no doubt hard to understand. It was totally against reason. But Elijah was obedient and he went to the brook Cherith, "according to the word of the Lord." When we receive a word from God, we can stand on it, even though we do not necessarily understand it. This is God's required prerequisite for us.

I suppose this is the core of the problem in many Christian lives today—lack of obedience. God tells us to do a certain thing, to meet him in a certain place, and unlike Elijah, we rise up in defiance, arguing with God. Or we delay his call, procrastinate, put it off. Or perhaps we doubt him and really do not believe that he is the same today as he was in Elijah's day. The truth is, the God of most of us is too restricted to be the God of the Bible. Is it any wonder that there are so few men and women of God at the Cheriths today?

This is God's required prerequisite. With him obedience always comes first. As we are obedient he then will reveal the next step for us!

Fourth, at the brook Cherith we not only see God's recognized plan, God's restricted promise, God's required prerequisite, but:

GOD'S RELEASED PROVISION
(1 Kings 17:6)

After God's recognized plan (hiding at some brook Cherith), and after God's restricted promise (being in the middle of his will), and after God's required prerequisite (obedience), God released his provision upon Elijah. "And the ravens brought him bread and meat in the morning and bread and meat in the evening, and he would drink from the brook" (1 Kings 17:6). Elijah was alone, the companion of a few animals in the bottom of a gorge beside the little brook. As he looked up between the towering cliffs, he could see a little patch of blue sky. And yonder, from above, came the ravens bearing in their beaks bread and meat for the prophet. Here we see God being faithful to his word due to conditions met by his man.

Many wonder why they don't live with the provisions of God. The reasons have never been more obvious than in this text—(1) lack of a place of prayer; (2) lack of being in the will of God; (3) lack of obedience to the call of God! Upon Elijah's obedience and surrender to God's will, "the ravens brought him bread and meat in the morning and bread and meat in the evening, and he would drink from the brook." The provisions of God were released upon him! But, had he not been obedient and pulled apart to hide, and had he not hid "there" at Cherith, he would have missed the plenteous provisions of God.

Thus, we see here that God is faithful! We can trust the Lord. God is waiting, willing, and longing to release his provisions upon the obedience of any of his children to his own perfect will.

And finally, at the brook we see:

GOD'S REVEALED PURPOSE
(1 Kings 17:7)

Some God this is! We can hardly believe what we read in this seventh verse. After all, he tells Elijah to go to the brook

Cherith and he will provide for him there. Elijah moves in obedience to the place only to find that "it happened after a while, that the brook dried up, because there was no rain in the land!" (1 Kings 17:7). The running brook dried up! No more water! Why would this great God allow such a thing to happen? Here God was revealing his purpose. Elijah's heart was being tested to see if his trust was in the brook Cherith or in the living God!

Many of us are called upon to sit by some drying brook. Perhaps the drying brook of health, or money, or friendships, or any number of hundreds of other brooks. It is easier to face the prophets of Baal on some Mount Carmel than to sit by some drying brook Cherith.

Why does God allow the brook to dry up on his children? He wants to teach us not to trust in his gifts but in himself! He longs to drain us of self that we might honor and acknowledge him as Lord of all! We must never be guilty of trusting in our Cherith in place of the living God. I fear this is a problem with many of us today. We are so likely to trust in our blessings to the near exclusion of genuine trust in the blesser himself.

What will God do when the brook dries up? When his purpose with us "there" is accomplished? Review the very next verses. "Then the word of the Lord came to him saying, 'Arise, go to Zarephath, which belongs to Sidon, and stay there; behold I have commanded a widow there to provide for you' " (1 Kings 17:8-9). God just leads us on to higher ground! Go on up to Zarephath. Obedience is the key, trusting him to take us one step at a time!

I never cease to be fascinated by the awesome, powerful Atlantic Ocean that borders my city on the east. The surface of that great ocean is never still. The tides are in constant motion. Those who live near the ocean know that the tide comes in twice each day. During its rise, the tide is called the flood tide. Then during its fall, it is called ebb tide. Henry Wadsworth Longfellow once noted, "The lowest ebb is the turn of the tide."

Perhaps, my friend, you find yourself at some dry brook—the tide has gone out. It is in fact the ebb tide of your life. Don't give up! Get in, and go on! Have faith. The lowest ebb is the turn of the tide. And this is true not only of the seas but of life. God is all the while revealing his purpose to you.

So, you are interested in becoming a man of God? Then "Go away from here and turn eastward, and hide yourself by the brook Cherith, which is east of the Jordan. And it shall be that you shall drink of the brook, and I have commanded the ravens to provide for you there" (1 Kings 17:3-4). I call you today to go there, to Cherith. I do not know where your Cherith is, but God knows and will lead you there and meet you there! Once there you will see God's recognized plan, God's restricted promise, God's required prerequisite, God's released provision, and God's revealed purpose. He will meet your needs. He will bless you, He will meet you. He will prepare you for some Mount Carmel. He will lead you. And if while there the brook begins to run dry, just remember this is God's method of teaching you to trust totally in him and not in your brook. There must be a Cherith to fit us all for Carmel in the making of men and women for God. Therefore, arise and go there today. The brook Cherith is an integral part in the making of a servant of God.

We have come once again to the end of a volume. It can be the continuation of a victorious walk with God as you enter in and go on with Jesus, *after revival comes.*